STOP LIVING ON AUTOPILOT

Take Responsibility for Your Life and Rediscover a Bolder, Happier You

ANTONIO NEVES

RODALE BOOKS
NEW YORK

Published in the United States by Rodale Books, an imprint of Random
House, a division of Penguin Random House LLC, New York.

rodalebooks.com

RODALE and the Plant colophon are registered trademarks of
Penguin Random House LLC.

Library of Congress Cataloging-in-Publication Data
Names: Neves, António, author.
Title: Stop living on autopilot : take responsibility for your life and
rediscover a bolder, happier you / Antonio Neves.
Description: New York : Rodale Books, 2021. | Includes index.
Identifiers: LCCN 2020019565 | ISBN 9780593136836 (hardcover) |
ISBN 9780593136850 (trade paperback) | ISBN 9780593136843
(ebook)
Subjects: LCSH: Self-actualization (Psychology) | Happiness.
Classification: LCC BF637.S4 N467 2021 | DDC 158--dc23
LC record available at https://lccn.loc.gov/2020019565

ISBN 978-0-593-13683-6
Ebook ISBN 978-0-593-13684-3

Printed in the United States of America

Book design by Jen Valero
Jacket design by Pete Garceau
Jacket photograph by Mark Leibowitz

10   9   8   7   6   5   4   3   2   1

First Edition

For my family, Brigitte, August, and Harper

CONTENTS

▶ START HERE

HOW THE HELL *did I end up here?*

This is the question you might ask yourself when you look in a mirror and attempt to evaluate where you are (or aren't) in life. If you're honest with yourself, you can acknowledge that things haven't felt right for quite some time. Kind of like a shoe that fits but is half a size too small. It's very possible that you've been in a funk far longer than you care to admit.

Maybe you've found yourself at the metaphorical fork in the road of life and when you evaluate your options of going left or right, you're strongly starting to consider plowing straight ahead instead.

At times like these you might ask yourself:

"Why am I so unhappy?"

"How did I gain all of this weight?"

"Why didn't I ever move to another city?"

"How did I end up in a marriage where all we do is argue?"

"Why am I still at this job that I hate?"

"Why are my kids behaving like jerks?"

"How did I end up living check to check?"

"How did I end up divorced and a single parent?"

"Why did I buy that time-share?"

"When did I start collecting fast-food condiments in my glove compartment?"

Or if you're anything like me in 2016—when things were allegedly going *great* in my life—the question could look more like this:

How did I end up "successful"... and yet I'm still miserable?

If you Googled my name back in 2016, the results would've made it seem like I was living my best life ever and that I had it all figured out. According to the Internet I was:

- A leadership speaker who delivered keynotes across the globe at top companies like Google.

- An award-winning broadcast journalist who spent more than ten years working with major television networks, including NBC, Nickelodeon, and BET.

- An Ivy League graduate.

- An executive coach to business leaders.

- An author of three successful self-published books.

- A former kids' television show host.

- A social media–verified public figure with that little blue check mark on Facebook and Twitter.

- A contributor to major online business outlets, including *Inc.com* and *Entrepreneur.com*.

- *A former Division I NCAA student-athlete.*
- *A husband and father of healthy boy and girl twins.*

All of those things were true. It may have seemed like I had a storybook life and career. But here's the thing: Google and social media only tell part of our story. The Internet can never tell the *whole* story.

The *real* story, the one I didn't talk about or publicly share, was that I was at a low point in my life. I was regularly experiencing more failures and setbacks than I cared to count.

What Google wouldn't have told you in 2016 was that:

- *After just a year of marriage, my wife and I were knee-deep in marriage counseling.*
- *Our twins arrived at thirty-two weeks and spent a month in the neonatal intensive care unit.*
- *Due to emotional eating, I had gained nearly thirty pounds and grew a big beard to hide my weight gain (which didn't disguise it one bit).*
- *After one too many visits to the hospital emergency room, I was wearing a heart monitor and undergoing cardiac MRIs and stress tests.*
- *My evenings were spent wallowing in self-misery, drinking tequila, whiskey, and wine (thankfully not at the same time).*
- *I started buying and carrying pocketknives for absolutely no good reason at all.*
- *I had a ridiculous amount of graduate school debt.*
- *I started avoiding family and friends, not returning their calls, texts, or e-mails.*
- *When I delivered keynotes, I was going through the motions on stages in front of hundreds and sometimes thousands of people.*

- At times, I found myself behaving like a child, based on the whims of my emotions, instead of like an adult, based on standards and values.

- My father's dementia was quickly advancing and we could no longer have those father-and-son conversations that I previously took for granted.

- To top it off, I regularly smoked Camel Crush Menthol cigarettes (yep, the ones where you click a crushable capsule to activate the menthol) in street alleys while wearing a bright green gardening glove so my wife wouldn't smell the stench on my hand.

Yeah, the Internet didn't tell the whole story. Not even close. At the time, I was living two lives—one of outward success and the other of inward turmoil, anxiety, and fear.

LOSING MY SPIRIT

The truth is that I felt lost, stuck, and horribly out of place in my own life, even after achieving most of the things I thought I wanted to accomplish. Even more, I felt burnt out, broken down, and washed up at a time when I needed to maintain my A game for my family.

Like most Americans (according to a Gallup[1] poll), I felt more depressed, personally and professionally, and dissatisfied with my life than ever before. Even though I knew I had a lot of life to live, I felt like I was past my prime. Like I had missed my chance to do something great.

Although I once greeted each day with a smile and a spirit of optimism, my go-getter attitude had been replaced with a constant frown of pessimism. I guess you could say I was losing my spirit. My immediate solution for this internal crisis was to take a hands-off approach and accept almost zero responsibility for where life had led me. I had transitioned to autopilot instead of living life with intention and purpose. Slowly but surely, I was morphing into what one day could become a bitter old man.

Of course, this wasn't the first time that I'd struggled in my life—far from it. In my twenties and thirties, while working for major television networks in New York City as a host, correspondent, and producer, I was tested in ways I'd never imagined. Still, 2016 felt different. Previously, when things didn't go my way, I believed that I had time and youth on my side. But now that I was in my forties, things didn't seem as simple. I was older—and even had a few gray hairs on my chin to show for it. I had a wife, kids, a minivan, and a growing list of responsibilities.

The irony was that what I was experiencing couldn't have been more removed from what my family, friends, and social media followers believed about me. To them, my life was a clear-cut success. How would they know any differently? In a world where we curate our lives to fit a specific narrative for everyone to see, it's harder than ever to admit when we're struggling. My offline life, my *real* life, felt like a game of tug-of-war—and I was the rope.

The former optimist in me was now convinced that the best thing to ever happen to me was over and in my past. It felt like my glory days were behind me. I started to tell myself that moving forward, my life wasn't going to be the fairy tale that I had once envisioned. What I didn't know at the time was that sometimes when you're lost, you actually get the opportunity to find yourself.

"YOU GOTTA FIGURE THAT SHIT OUT"

There were days in 2016 when I was right. I hadn't "lived up to my potential." I wasn't the man I thought I'd be. One day, when I was smoking one of those Camel Crush Menthol cigarettes in a Santa Monica street alley, a homeless man asked me if he could bum a cigarette. It was obvious that he'd seen better days, so I gave him a few.

After he lit his cigarette, he asked me about the bright green gardening glove I was wearing. When I explained to him that I wore it to hide the smoke smell from my unsuspecting wife, he looked at me as if he felt sorry for me.

He took a slow drag and matter-of-factly said, "Hey man. You gotta figure that shit out." Then, he walked away. That moment crushed me more than the Camels.

That brief encounter, simple as it was, set me on a mission to course-correct my life. The pendulum had swung to both extremes: following a path of conformity, or almost falling off the edge. It was time to stop running away from life, and face what I was experiencing head-on. It was time to come back to the middle.

The journey started with a series of difficult questions, all of which I'll share with you in this book. Along the way, I came to realize that my dreams had an expiration date. If I didn't act on them, they would be lost forever.

LIFE ISN'T SHORT

There's nothing extraordinary about the struggle that I experienced. No one was going to feel sorry for me, nor should they.

People have experienced far worse. I ended up where I was based on the decisions I did (and didn't) make.

Millions of people have stories like mine. Exhibiting outward success while hiding private angst. Over the years, many of these people would come up to me after my talks at conferences. Somehow, despite there being an abundance of life coaches out there, these people would find and hire me—and share their stories with me. They'd often bare their souls to me via e-mail, looking for a way to reverse their own downslide.

Like many coaches, I have a gift for helping people solve the same problems and navigate the same challenges that I'm personally encountering. That's when I learned that my own experiences, as challenging as they were, had served a valuable purpose: they were my University of Life. They gave me a gift as a speaker, coach, and trainer that could help others transition during challenging periods in their lives. This realization gave me a new lease on life.

People like to say, "Life is short." But as the comedian Chris Rock brilliantly said in a comedy special, "Some people say life is short, and that you could get hit by a bus at any moment, and that you have to live each day like it's your last. Bullshit. Life is long. You're probably not gonna get hit by a bus. And you're gonna have to live with the choices you make for the next fifty years."

Amen. Life can be long. And one day, we'll want to look back on our life and marvel at everything we experienced instead of wondering in a daze, *What happened?*

In fact, the question "What happened?" is one of my greatest fears. When I'm at my worst, I envision bumping into someone I knew from years ago. After a short conversation, they'd look me directly in the eyes and notice that the zest for life they'd once seen in me had disappeared and was now replaced with indifference. They would walk away saying, "What happened to that guy?"

Of course, what they're really asking is, "Why did he give up?"

But this book isn't about giving into our worst fears. It's about learning how to embrace them and to recommit to our dreams and reimagine our future. To remember that we have a say in our lives.

WHAT TO EXPECT FROM THIS BOOK

If your life is a constant battle between two narratives—one of outwardly meeting (maybe even exceeding) expectations and another of inwardly battling turmoil—this book is for you.

This book wasn't written in a cabin, in the middle of the woods, at a writer's retreat while my life, family, and responsibilities were put on hold (though, believe me, I would've loved that). No, I wrote it in the midst of real life, happening in real time with all the ups, downs, hurdles, and complications that come with it. This, I've found, is where the truth lives.

Over the years, I've come to learn that we all have the answers to our most pressing problems and challenges. It's just that we haven't been asked the right questions. That's what this book will provide: targeted and perhaps uncomfortable questions for you to consider at the moment you most need them. Your answers might surprise you and will allow you to shift your life in the direction of your choosing.

There will be questions that can make you uneasy.

Questions that could make you laugh.

Questions that might make you cry.

Questions that will provide answers to serve as a road map

on your journey forward to help you reimagine not just today, but also your future.

To be very clear, this book isn't about quitting your job or taking a sabbatical to Bali to discover your passion, meaning, and purpose. It's not about getting a raise or promotion. And it's not about moving into a bigger house on the other side of town. All of those are cop-outs. A new job, more money, or fancier zip code can't save you. Only you can.

This book is instead about committing and recommitting to what's most important in your everyday life. It's about creating purpose and meaning in your life as opposed to looking for it. It's about being real, honest, and accountable so you can live boldly and courageously as you once did before the roadblocks of life got in your way. All while keeping your sense of wonder, humor, and curiosity.

Part One of this book will help you unpack the choices you made and identify how you got where you are today.

Part Two will start you on the path of building accountability and a strong foundation to begin the transition to the life you desire. It will provide you with steps to take to ignite lasting change.

On the following pages, you'll find exercises and activities that I've designed and used on stages, in workshops, with private-coaching clients, and with myself. They work. But for you to see actual results, you must do the work. I've come to learn that most transformations and spiritual journeys aren't always enjoyable, even if they're necessary.

The great news is that everything you've experienced in your life up to this point—all your wins, losses, successes, and failures—has shaped you into the brilliant and resilient human being you are today. All of this has prepared you for what you're about to do next. I'm genuinely excited for you.

Now that we got that out of the way, let's get a few things straight:

In real life, there are no movie montages where everything is magically fixed in sixty seconds. Change happens in real time.

No one owes you anything. You owe yourself everything.

No matter where you stand today, your story isn't over yet. A new chapter begins right now.

No one can, or will, care more about your life than you do. So, it's time to start acting like it.

The best thing to happen to you hasn't happened yet.

Now let's get to work. Your time isn't coming. It's here.

PART ONE

THE FIRST DAY OF THE REST OF YOUR LIFE

THE BEST THING

"Keep some room in your heart for the unimaginable."

—MARY OLIVER, PULITZER PRIZE–WINNING POET

IT'S IN THE quiet moments that our voice can speak to us the loudest. Although rarely is it what we want to hear.

These are the moments when we awake before the sun rises and we're alone with our thoughts. It's when someone who knows us well asks a deep question, so deep that we can't immediately answer. And, it's when we see ourselves in the mirror for what seems like the very first time.

It's then that we tell ourselves a version of the same story.

One day, I found myself in a completely different situation than I had imagined for myself . . .

Out of the blue, my relationship was in shambles . . .

Suddenly, I realized that I hated my job . . .

Telling ourselves stories like these is far easier than accepting a painful and sobering truth.

"One day" is actually a large collection of days.

"Out of the blue" is seldom a surprise.

And, "Suddenly" is rarely sudden.

The hard-to-accept truth is that the life you find yourself in today wasn't created overnight. Your journey has been a *process*—a string of decisions you've made, rather than one single defining moment. All of this is compounded by silenced doubts and ignored intuitions.

As author, researcher, and all-around awesome thinker Brené Brown once wrote, "The universe is not short on wake-up calls. We're just quick to hit the snooze button."

These days, when sports teams use the mantra "Trust the process" or career politicians use the phrase "Stay the course," I have to take a deep breath. Both mottos nod to staying committed to the decisions that we've made, which is innocent enough. However, I always want to add, "Before you trust the process and stay the course, make sure it's the *right* process and the *right* course."

If you're at a place in life where things are no longer making sense the way they once did, don't worry. You're at the right place. Consider this book your wake-up call.

PLAYING BY THE RULES HAS LET YOU DOWN

So, let's answer the question: how did you get here? The irony is that for all intents and purposes, you've likely done *everything* that society, your parents, teachers, and elders told you to do to be successful and happy.

You played by the rules. You chased challenges, checking off boxes year after year. You got your education. You got a good job. You didn't get arrested (or at least you've had that misdemeanor expunged by now). You practiced safe sex (except that one time). You donate every now and then to charitable organizations (even if it's just for tax purposes). Maybe you are even married or in a good relationship—or at least have experienced one. Hell, you may even have a full-on family, house, garage, dog, and yard. What's true is that your friends, family, colleagues, and strangers on social media probably consider your life to be a screaming success. It looks like you have it all figured out.

All of this may seem cool, but the truth is that you don't feel nearly as happy as you look on Instagram or as successful as you present yourself to be on LinkedIn. The simple yet challenging thing to admit is that you don't have it all figured out. Not even close. To top it all off, odds are that more is expected of you than ever before. From your home to your office, people—your family, friends, and colleagues—count on you.

The stress and anxiety you feel these days is real. Not only do you feel unfulfilled, but you're also starting to question every decision you've ever made. The college you attended. The city you live in. The job you accepted. The relationship you're in. The name of your child. The money you loaned to your cousin that you know you'll never see again. That horrible time-share in Hawaii you invested in after drinking too many Mai Tais that you can't sell to save your life. That damn tattoo (and wow, do I have a tattoo story for you later).

When you dig deeper, what you're really questioning are the times you played it safe. The moments when you ignored your gut. The instances when you ran away from what was most important to you and didn't shoot your shot.

What it boils down to is that you're starting to feel out of place in your own life. It's been like this for a while and it's starting to scare you.

On most days, you do a relatively good job playing the role of "adult." You pay your bills on time. You do the work that's asked of you at your job. You handle your household duties. You listen to your significant other talk about their day. You get the next round of drinks for your friends. You eat relatively well, except when no one is watching. You get your oil changed before the light comes on. You even do a courtesy flush.

However, your once-rosy outlook on life is slowly being replaced by incoming clouds of pessimism. You've become more focused on "What if it doesn't work out?" as opposed to "What if it does work out?"

Your new normal is feeling like a can of soda that's been shaken for too long and is on the verge of exploding (of course, while you're wearing all white). You don't know if you'll explode today, tomorrow, next week, or next month. But whoever will be on the receiving end of that magnificent explosion—whether it's your spouse, kids, colleague, roommate, random guy seated next to you on an airplane, or grocery store clerk—they probably don't deserve your ire.

I know exactly what it feels like to be on the verge of exploding. Hell, I even know what it feels like to explode at the absolute worst possible times (more on that later). Been there, done that. Bought the T-shirt. The good news is that I also know what it's like to chart a new path and positively transform my life for the better. So have countless others who I've coached, worked with, and interviewed over the years.

Does this mean that my life today is always filled with sunshine and healthy organic food, and that everything is "amazing"? Hell, no. This isn't an Instagram story. What it does mean is that I live life on purpose instead of by accident.

So, what's the secret? I'm glad you asked. Let me tell you a short story.

THE BEST THING

Back in 2006, there was a big college football game. It was the BCS National Championship Game between the University of

Southern California Trojans and the University of Texas Long-horns.

USC entered the game with a thirty-four-game winning streak, and they had two of the best players in the country. Almost no one picked Texas to win the game. They were the underdog. The media billed it as David versus Goliath.

But that night, in front of nearly 94,000 people at the Rose Bowl and with 35 million people watching on televisions across the country, something amazing happened in Pasadena, California. You probably already figured this out, but the University of Texas won the football game and proved the naysayers wrong.

Like most, I love a great underdog story. However, this story goes much deeper. In the locker room after the game, as the University of Texas players were celebrating, their head coach, Mack Brown, arrived to give his post-game speech.

In keeping with tradition, Brown congratulated the players for winning the national championship. Then, he said something that the people in the locker room probably will never forget:

"I don't want this to be the best thing that's ever happened to you," he said. "When you're fifty-four, I don't want you to say, 'Winning a football game was the best thing that ever happened in my life.' You'll have it. And you'll be a champion for the rest of your life. You make sure that's one of the best *sports* things in your life."

Wow. These young men were fresh from winning a national championship and their coach tells them to make sure that something *better* happens in their lives. Damn right. This story is an important reminder not to focus so much on what we did in the past that we lose sight of what's possible today and in the future.

So, what does this football story have to do with you? Well, call me silly, but I believe that the best thing to ever happen to you is *ahead* of you—not behind you. The secret: when you start to believe this, everything begins to change.

For you to believe this, for it to be real, it requires a major shift in perspective. A shift that won't happen overnight.

It requires a straightforward, direct, and unapologetic approach to life. An approach focused on the right mindset, beliefs, and way of life.

It requires making decisions and taking actions every single day long after the motivation has gone away and even when you don't feel like it.

It requires remembering that the major moments in our lives are just that—moments that fit into the bigger journey of who we're striving to become.

It requires our dreams to be bigger than our complaints.

It requires taking ownership to accept that each day is a blank canvas upon which we can create what we choose—from this day forward. You are the artist.

Based on where you are in life right now, I know this might seem a bit naïve. Kind of like something that someone who believes in unicorns might say. However, unless you're Neil Armstrong and have already walked on the moon, I believe that the odds of your future being brighter than your past are in your favor—regardless of what you've experienced. When you commit to believing that the best is ahead of you, it will light a spark and rekindle that fire that has always been burning deep inside you, leading you to a brighter future.

Call it faith. Call it magic. Call it crazy. Simply put, when you believe and behave as if the best is still ahead of you, your outlook on life and behaviors immediately begin to change, too.

To achieve what you want to achieve, sometimes you have to believe what others don't.

Because you're reading this book, I know that there's more life inside of you to live. There are more great days ahead. There's much more to give. As long as you're breathing, your tank isn't empty. Believe me, I know.

THE BREAKFAST OF CHAMPIONS

If someone told me back in September 2004 that a brighter future was ahead of me, I probably would've punched them in the esophagus. Because my life at that time was pure misery.

At the time, I lived on the second floor of an ugly green apartment building at the end of a dead-end street in the Silver Lake neighborhood of Los Angeles. Though Silver Lake was quickly becoming a popular hipster neighborhood, the street I lived on had yet to receive the press release.

The apartment building hallways always smelled like cigarette smoke, mold, and oddly, baked goods. My neighbors were a combination of wannabe actors and people who stayed at home all day doing something (though I didn't know exactly what).

In my dingy, sparsely furnished apartment, I regularly sat on the floor inside a small utility closet. The door was always closed. The lights were off. I didn't want to see the world, and I didn't want the world to see me. In the midst of the darkness, all I saw was the occasional amber glow of the joints I would smoke.

It was always hot. Hot enough to turn on the air-conditioning. But the AC just pumped out lukewarm air, so I always had my shirt off. My former almost-six-pack of abs had morphed into an official six-pack of flab. Not the progress I'd hoped for at that point in my life.

Most days my routine involved taking deep hits of weed and drinking Pabst Blue Ribbon beer—both before 10:00 a.m. It was what I called my "breakfast of champions." My greatest joy back then? A DVD arriving in the mail from Netflix.

During this spell, I hardly worked. To pay my bills, I collected an unemployment check every couple of weeks. When I did "work," I participated in off-the-books focus groups in a large corporate building where Santa Monica Boulevard meets the 405 Freeway.

In the focus groups, I quickly learned to say yes to everything. Saying yes could mean the difference between earning twenty dollars and eighty dollars. "Will you purchase a riding lawn mower in the next year?" Absolutely. (Who cares that I live in a second-floor apartment?) "Are you currently ovulating?" Bet your ass I am.

Not far from my apartment was the world-famous HOLLYWOOD sign in the Santa Monica Mountains. The sign provided daily inspiration to even the most untalented actors and writers, helping them believe that they still had a shot. However, I might as well have been in Cleveland because I spent most of my days in my closet or on my bed or couch. I wasn't looking for inspiration. The sign was the last thing I wanted to see because it was a reminder—of what was and what could've been.

THIS IS WHAT IT'S LIKE TO BE "SOMEBODY"

Just a few months earlier, I had my dream job. People knew who I was. By "people," I mean kids between the ages of six and twelve years old (and their mothers).

Every weekday, kids across the country could turn on their TVs and tune into Nickelodeon to watch me on the daily sketch show *U-Pick Live*. It was broadcast from the tenth floor of 1515 Broadway (upstairs from MTV's *Total Request Live*) in the heart of New York City's Times Square.

The cast included the two main cohosts: a beautiful dirty-blonde woman who was a former junior gymnastics champion and a geeky skinny guy who wore thick glasses. There was a superhero, Pick Boy, who wore an ill-fitting costume of tights, a mask, and a cape. There also was a cow and an out-of-shape wrestler. And then there was me—the hip, ethnically vague black guy with dreadlocks.

Though I first started working on the show in 2002 as a production assistant, I quickly found my way on camera. What started as periodic appearances transitioned to becoming a full-on day player with a talent contract. Sometimes I even had the opportunity to cohost the show with the superhero when the main hosts were at special events.

Sketches were written just for me, including "Antonio's Floating Head" and the Evel Knievel knockoff "Wildtonio," where I wore an all-white jumpsuit and performed not-so-amazing feats on Rollerblades or skateboards in tight hallways. I even had my own unoriginal catchphrase: "All right!"

On a weekly basis, I regularly spent time on camera and behind the scenes with the major stars who appeared on our show to promote their latest projects: Beyoncé, Will Ferrell, Anthony Anderson, Adam Sandler, Kelly Clarkson, Jack Black, and Jennifer Garner, to name a few.

Every day, I signed autographs for kids in the audience, on the street, or at random places like airports and at New York Mets baseball games. And yes, I pursued and was pursued by moms who knew me as "that guy on Nickelodeon my kids watch." I felt like I'd made it.

To top it off, I was making more money than I ever had

before in my life. Not Oprah money. Not banker money. Not even I-cohost-a-show-on-a-cable-network money. But it was more than enough to start saving, open a mutual fund account with astronomical maintenance fees, and buy rounds of beers for my friends at the bar.

This is what it's like to be somebody, I started to believe after a couple of years. This feeling didn't last long. When life knocked me down in 2004, it didn't hold back. The day it all came crashing down, I was completely and totally unprepared.

The executive producer of *U-Pick Live*'s words hit me like a swinging kettlebell to my scrotum:

"The show is going in a different direction," he said. "We're not going to bring you back as a cohost."

To say that I was stunned by being fired would be a gross understatement. I didn't immediately respond to the executive producer's words and I did all I could to hold back my tears. All I could think was that kids would never hear me say my catchphrase, "All right!" ever again. Even worse, they probably wouldn't even notice that I was gone.

I wanted to scream, "How can this show go on without a black guy with dreads? Every talk show, sitcom, newscast, and kids' program has a black guy. *I'm the black guy!*" But I didn't. Because the truth was, they didn't need me.

Admittedly, the past year on the show hadn't been exactly amazing, thanks in part to my burgeoning ego. At one point during the previous season, thanks to my Leo pride, I refused to appear on the show until a contract situation was resolved. Remember: on good days, I was the *fourth* person on the cast totem pole. I wasn't the reason kids tuned into the show, but I acted like it.

Also, during that season, things outside of the show started to happen for me. I landed a development deal with Nickelodeon for a live-action show I created called *Oh Brotha!* I was the periodic voice of the now-defunct Nickelodeon Games and Sports (GaS) for Kids channel, recording lines like "Coming up next on Nick GaS is Legends of the Hidden Temple." I even hosted a pilot for an improv comedy show for Nickelodeon's sister network, the N, with the actors Paul Scheer and Colton Dunn. In short, I was more distracted and unfocused than ever, and I wasn't willing to put in the work required to perform at a high level. Though I wasn't mature enough to see it at the time, I played a major role in my own crash.

Shell-shocked, I left the Nickelodeon headquarters in Times Square. I took the N train to Astoria, my neighborhood in Queens, stopping by the local video rental store on my way home. I immediately went to the back section with the black curtain. I pulled that curtain back with a vengeance. I rented not one, but two adult films. This was the beginning of my downward spiral.

When I got home, I grabbed a pair of scissors. I looked in the mirror and, one by one, cut off each of my dreadlocks, which had taken more than four years to grow. I cried like a baby. My dreams, hopes, and ambitions were now in my past. All I had left to do was watch two adult films on VHS and wallow in self-pity.

Getting fired sent me on a months-long bender of feeling sorry for myself and seeking out substances instead of real support. Friends consoled me by saying, "Maybe it wasn't meant to be," but their words didn't help. It would've been easy to blame this on my boss, but upon closer examination, I realized this was a long time coming.

I fell apart. I was broke, depressed, and alone. Though I was still in my twenties, I thought the best thing to ever happen to me had passed me by. What I didn't know then is that:

*Sometimes
what seems like a
destination is actually
a bridge to a new chapter.*

WHERE YOU STAND TODAY

Since you're reading this, you've probably figured out that the Nickelodeon gig wasn't actually the best thing that ever happened to me, though it did teach me some valuable lessons.

Today, when I think back to my more recent days of smoking Camel Crush Menthol cigarettes in street alleys while wearing a bright green gardening glove, I remember feeling the exact same way all over again—like my best days were behind me. The good news is that I was wrong both times.

Right now, you may feel as if the best thing to ever happen is behind you and in your past—like I did on quite a few occasions in my life. If you're like most people, you've probably kept how you feel buried deep inside. Why? Because you think, *Who am I to complain?*

That is, until one day—the day you hoped would never come—you look in the mirror and realize you can no longer fake it. You truly see who you've become . . . and you hardly recognize that person.

You crave, want, and need change in your life. Your biggest fear is turning into one of those people who have given up on the promise of what life could offer if they just pursued their truth. You see the resignation in their postures and in their actions (or lack thereof). You see the defeat in the jobs they haven't left as they await "just one more bonus," and in their relationships. And you're worried that this could be you.

It's time to start breaking the rules that have led you down the wrong path. Think of it this way:

Tombstones could have three dates.
The day you were born. The day you gave up.
The day you died.

Sadly, people often lose far too many years between giving up and dying. But it doesn't have to be that way. You know this because you've seen those rare men and women who seem to know something that no one else does. Those people who seem to live life with purpose and zest. Those people who don't apologize or feel guilty for who they are and what they choose to pursue and stand for. It's not about money, status, or fame. It's about intention. You crave that life.

What you want is adventure. To be bold. To be courageous. To chase after meaning. To go against the norm. To piss people off. To have an opinion. To explore your sexual fetishes. To say what you actually mean out loud. To say no to all of the stuff you grudgingly say yes to. To feel like you have a say in your own life.

How do you know you crave change? Here are the signs:

It's the angst you feel when you first wake up in the morning. It's the fatigue you feel when you haven't done anything to earn that fatigue. It's going through the motions at work. It's feeling out of place among the people you know best. It's the lies you tell yourself and the actions you hide from others.

More than anything, it's the metaphorical tap on your shoulder saying, "This isn't it."

THE FIVE BEST THINGS

Before you start to think too much or feel too sorry for yourself, let's flip the script and interrupt your thought process. To do that, let's dig a bit into your past and what has come to define your years on this planet with an exercise. This may seem like a harsh transition, but sometimes harsh transitions are exactly what we need to wake us up from a trance that has been years in the making.

Get a piece of paper and write down the five best things to ever happen to you that have helped shape who you are today. I'll get it started by sharing mine from 2016, when I was going through a challenging time.

THE FIVE BEST THINGS TO EVER HAPPEN IN MY LIFE

1. *Getting married*

2. *Becoming the father of twins*

3. *Graduating from college*

4. *Moving into our new home*

5. *Earning a master's degree from Columbia University*

Now it's your turn. Write down the five best things that ever happened in your life.

1.

2.

3.

4.

5.

Great. We'll do this exercise again, but with a twist.

Now, write down the five best things to ever happen to you, but *don't* include graduating from college, getting married, having kids, or other traditional markers of success. We want to get more specific about what makes you, you. I'll get the party started.

THE FIVE BEST THINGS TO EVER HAPPEN TO ME (AND ONLY ME)

1. *Moving to New York City with about $800 in my bank account*

2. *Leaving my ten-year-long television career to start my own leadership and development company*

3. *Being a walk-on NCAA student-athlete*

4. *Hosting a leadership retreat in Nicaragua*

5. *Studying abroad in Spain*

Now it's your turn. Write down the five best things to ever happen to you without including major life milestones that revolve around others.

1.

2.

3.

4.

5.

How much overlap is there or isn't there with your answers? If you take a look at my answers, there isn't much.

My guess is that it was challenging for you to identify the "best things" when you didn't include graduating from college, getting married, having kids, or other major life events. If so, good. You're thinking. You're trying.

Why was this exercise challenging? Probably because no one has ever asked you this question framed that way. Sadly, it's rare for us to pause and reflect with simple, yet powerful questions like these—and sometimes, we all need a little coaching.

Now, let's dig even deeper. We've just scratched the surface. Take a look at that second list (the one that doesn't include traditional markers of success). Identify the primary feelings or emotions you felt when those things were happening. I'll start with mine:

1. *Moving to New York City with about $800 in my bank account—Fearful*

2. *Leaving my ten-year-long television career behind to start my own leadership and development company—Courageous*

3. *Being a walk-on NCAA student-athlete—Challenged*

4. *Hosting a leadership retreat in Nicaragua—Energized*

5. *Studying abroad in Spain—Excited*

You're up. What feelings or emotions were you experiencing at the time?

1.

2.

3.

4.

5.

The reason why it's important to identify the emotions that you were feeling at the time is that more often than not, what you're chasing in life isn't necessarily an event, a dream job, or the perfect soul mate.

What you're chasing in life is a feeling.
A feeling that reminds you that you're alive.

WHAT ARE YOU MOVING TOWARD?

Here are some important and powerful questions to ponder and answer as you move forward:

Based on your current path in life, what are you moving toward?

Is what you're moving toward a future you desire, or one that will break your heart? Why?

When I answered these questions for myself during my crisis in 2016, it broke my heart—partly because, after crashing and burning in my twenties at the beginning of my television career, I thought I'd figured it all out.

My answers revealed that I was moving toward having health complications from my crappy eating, alcohol consuming, and cigarette smoking to combat stress and anxiety. My marriage was moving toward friction, turmoil, and resentment. My relationship with our infant twins was defined more by disconnection than connection. My career felt like it was starting to regress when my family needed my support the most.

If my reality at the time had progressed into the future, it would have broken my heart because I could have lost everything that mattered to me. And the fear of losing what I love made me realize that I wasn't fully showing up for myself, my family, and my work. "Good enough" was no longer good enough.

Now that you know more about my personal life than some

of my family members, it's your turn. Set a timer and spend five minutes answering these questions:

> *Based on your current path in life, what are you moving toward?*
>
> *Is what you're moving toward a future you desire or one that will break your heart? Why?*

Though challenging, writing down your honest answers will help reveal your path forward. Don't think too much. Don't lie. Don't judge what you write. Don't self-edit. Just answer straight from your heart. No chaser. Just write.

Based on what you wrote, if you're honestly headed toward a future that's better, good for you. Put down this book, find the nearest Jet Ski, and go ride on a lake.

If it's not ideal or if it's even worse, roll up your sleeves. You've got work to do. If it's par for the course, keep reading—because in my book, staying where you are can be a form of quitting.

Let's take these next steps to unpack these seminal moments in your life, and where you are today, to start the process of determining how they can help you take a step forward.

NEXT STEPS

1. Take a look at the second list you created of the five best things to ever happen in your life. What decisions allowed each of these things to happen?

2. What emotions did you feel when these things were happening? When is the last time you felt these emotions?

3. Based on your current path in life, what are you moving toward?

4. Is what you're moving toward a future you desire or one that will break your heart? Why?

YOUR LAST THIRTY DAYS

*"Man stands in his own shadow and
wonders why it's dark."*

—ZEN PROVERB

THERE'S A REASON why I ended the last chapter by asking if your life is moving toward a future that will break your heart. That's because in this chapter, I'm going to ask some more powerful questions about where your life is headed.

What I've come to learn is that when the right question shows up at the right time and place, it can start you on the path to transforming your life.

During my years as a leadership speaker and coach, I've asked one particular question to audiences and clients that always stops them in their tracks. It's the rare question that translates into all languages and resonates with people from all cultures and faiths. The question gets directly to the core of what it means to be the best, worst, or average version of ourselves. It pulls no punches. It takes no prisoners.

The first time I asked this question at a training and development event for a large international company in Amsterdam, I immediately knew I was onto something. The room went silent. People who were previously engaged and making eye contact with me diverted their gaze. The audience started to shift uncomfortably in their seats. There was a smattering of laughter amid a shocking silence. The energy in the room felt awkward, raw, charged, and anxious all at the same time.

Here's the question framed three different ways:

1. *Based on your last thirty days of work, if your company had to decide whether or not to rehire you, would they?*

2. *Based on your last thirty days of marriage (or whatever relationship you're in), would your partner immediately recommit to you?*

3. *Based on your last thirty days as a parent (if you are a parent), would your children want you to continue to be their parent?*

Reading these questions may make you want to put down this book or distract yourself with something unimportant like browsing social media, cleaning out your refrigerator, or researching different brands of waffle makers. But please keep reading. These questions are uncomfortable in the way that a massage can be a bit too hard, yet you're still eager to work through the knots and rough patches that have been causing you pain.

Now, be honest with yourself and really think about your last thirty days on this planet. Based on those last thirty days, would you get a firm vote of confidence, an immediate commitment, from the people in your life who matter most?

The easy, lazy answer to these questions is "Absolutely!" If that's your truth, great—but I don't believe you. That's because it's in our nature to seek comfort and to start taking life, work, and family for granted.

If you're being real with yourself, you might have a sinking feeling that based on your last thirty days at work, you really haven't been putting your best foot forward. Right now, whether your company would rehire you is probably a big question mark.

You might realize that based on your last thirty days, you've been taking your relationship for granted, putting your energy and focus toward other things. Whether or not your partner would immediately recommit to you is up in the air.

And you might acknowledge that based on your last thirty days of parenting, you haven't always been as present or as patient as you'd like. Maybe you're wondering if your kids would even want you to pick them up from school.

The hard-to-accept fact is that if nothing changes in your life moving forward, it can eventually lead to getting fired, a relationship coming to an end, or serving as a terrible role model for the child you love. In short, it can lead to your life rotting from the inside.

Deep in your core, you know the answers to these questions. Odds are, the answers make you uncomfortable. Yet, you're reaching a point where you feel even more uncomfortable for not having spoken your truth for so long. On the flip side, it's also quite possible that you're questioning if you still want to work for your company. If you still want to be with your partner. Or, if you would go back and have kids again.

Of course, these questions can also be framed in a variety of ways outside of our careers, relationships, and parenting. They can be based on how we've treated our friendships, our physical or mental health, or even our personal finances over the past thirty days. Regardless, these questions are about how you choose to show up to what you committed to do—until you make a different commitment.

WHY JUST THIRTY DAYS?

Before we dig deeper into the thirty-day question, you may be wondering, *Why just thirty days?*

What I sometimes find challenging about the personal development and coaching world is how we've been trained to ask people where they would like to be three to five years from now.

> *"What's your five-year plan? Paint a vision of a future that you want.... Make a vision board of what you want to manifest.... Who do you want to be when you're old and gray after your second hip replacement surgery?"*

These questions are innocent enough and typically have great intentions. However, the question of the five-year plan can project many people too far into the future. So much so that it can paralyze our thinking, creativity, and ability to dream. When we're in that state, we can hardly paint a picture of the next five weeks, let alone the next five years.

Right now, look back at what you were doing five years ago. Five years ago, did you think you'd be where you are right now? I guarantee you didn't. If you did, odds are you're experienced in time travel.

In my experience, and to be practical, if you want to know where you're headed in your future, all you have to do is look at your past thirty days—and there you are. At any time we can review our last thirty days and evaluate what we are or aren't doing to help us get back on track. We must look back to know where we're heading, but not so much that we trip over the past. That's why we're using the metric of looking back on just thirty days.

It's important to remember that these questions aren't a judgment about your past. Rather, they're an honest acknowledgment. A tip of the hat. They simply provide an invitation to evaluate our behavior and how we choose to show up for our commitments where we've pledged professional time, personal time, love, energy, and effort. It's not so much an invitation to reinvent who you are, but rather an opportunity to reimagine who you can be.

Once we do this, and only then, can we take the steps to hit the "reset" button for the present and future.

SMELLING THE CORK

As we're beginning to establish, part of living is making decisions, accepting our mistakes, learning lessons along the way, and harnessing those hard-won lessons into the story of who we are. Still, how do we determine who we want to be? How can we examine our most recent day-to-day experiences to help guide our path forward? Let's start with a story about cheese and wine that's not really about either.

If you would've asked me as a kid what I want to be when I grew up, I definitely wouldn't have smiled and said, "I want to be a cheese salesman." But that's exactly what I found myself doing in South Florida after I graduated from Western Michigan University in the late 1990s with a marketing degree in hand.

I lived in a town called Hollywood, just south of Fort Lauderdale. At the ripe age of twenty-two, I was responsible for about twenty Winn-Dixie grocery stores and part of my job was selling cheese.

To all of my family and friends, I was living the American Dream. I had that "good job" everyone talks about, I was dating an amazing woman, and my family couldn't have been prouder of me. *I've made it,* I regularly thought. I was the first one in my family to earn a college degree and secure a white-collar job with benefits and a 401(k) plan, which meant the world to me. And get this—I even had a company car. A sexy white Ford Taurus.

To supplement my income during my days slinging cheese, I worked a second job in the evenings as a server at an Italian restaurant in Fort Lauderdale. The restaurant had a great name, Antonio's, and above-average Italian food.

Some nights, the restaurant was bustling. Other nights, the lack of customers made watching paint dry seem more appealing than working a slow shift. This lack of foot traffic meant major fluctuations in the tips I received. However, one thing that was consistent at the restaurant was the bar scene. While the servers' evenings tended to be hit or miss, the bartenders always seemed to do pretty well with tips, especially during happy hour.

I wanted to make the same kind of money as the bartenders, so I did what you do in that kind of predicament—you enroll in one of Fort Lauderdale's "premier" bartending schools, housed in a questionable neighborhood in a beat-up strip mall.

Our instructor, let's call him Vinny, was a New Yorker from Queens who spoke with a thick accent. He looked like a combo of Andrew Dice Clay and Joe Pesci. It was obvious that he knew his way behind the bar, and alcohol knew the way to his stomach—even during business hours.

Before we knew it, my classmates and I were behind a makeshift bar mixing drinks from bottles filled with water colored with food dye to mimic the hues of whiskey, rum, sour mix, sweet vermouth, and more. But the day we graduated to learning about wine is a day that I'll never forget.

To begin our wine lesson, our instructor asked the class a

straightforward question: "Why do you smell the cork when you open a bottle of wine?"

Not a hand went up. Everyone averted their eyes, including me. I knew absolutely nothing about wine. Slowly, one student started to raise his hand. Before his hand was fully extended, the instructor pointed to him and called out, "You!"

You could tell the student immediately regretted his decision. He took a deep breath and then said, "For the memories?"

"Speak louder," the instructor bellowed.

Gathering his confidence, the student said louder, "You smell the cork for . . . ," and then he briefly paused, ". . . the memories."

None of us knew if he was right or wrong. We collectively held our breath.

"For the *memories*," the instructor said, kindly with a smile. "For the *memories*. Nice."

The student who answered smiled and sat upright in his seat, beaming with pride.

It was right then that the instructor said, "For the *memories*. Did you hear this guy? For the *memories*. You know what? Wine don't give a damn about your memories!"

We were all shell-shocked.

"You smell the cork to see if the wine has spoiled. To see if it's good to drink," Vinny continued. "Not for the frickin' memories. Get a load of this guy and his *memories*."

Ah. You smell the cork to see if the wine is good or bad. Got it. But not for the memories.

So, what does a wine cork have to do with you? Well, when is the last time you smelled the cork of your life to see if it's still good? We smell the "cork of life" to know if it's still sweet—if our life is humming along smoothly—or if it stinks, having spoiled like a bad bottle of wine turned into expensive vinegar.

When you look at your life, consider these key areas from a "life-coaching wheel":

- *Relationships*
- *Career*
- *Health*
- *Finances*
- *Family*

Is it all working? Has your approach to life worked in your favor or to your detriment? Is your life "good to drink" or should you pour it down the drain and purchase a new bottle? Only you know deep inside if it's working or not.

When I looked at my jobs in South Florida, selling cheese and serving Italian food, I realized that things had gone bad.

The irony is that I was relatively good at my job selling cheese. That's when I first began to learn the tough lesson that most of us tend to ignore:

Just because you're good at something, doesn't mean you're supposed to be doing it.

Deep inside, I knew that eventually I'd have to do something drastic. I was never willing to try cocaine, so I had to figure something else out. It's amazing what you're willing to do when life doesn't go the way you had planned and you're forced to make a decision.

Now, let's smell the cork in your life. If we pull back the curtain on the last thirty days, what will we discover? What went bad—what has stopped working in your life? The reason why I started asking audiences these questions is because I was really asking them of myself. So, let's dive in.

THE LAST THIRTY DAYS OF WORK

When I looked back on the year 2016 over a number of thirty-day stretches, my life was a hot mess consisting of health challenges, marital woes, stumbles through fatherhood, cigarette smoking in alleys, and personal setbacks. And things weren't any better with my career. When it came to my company and if they'd rehire me, the answer was a resounding no. The funny (not so funny) thing was that I was my own boss.

The disadvantage of running your own business is that there isn't always a guaranteed paycheck every two weeks. Benefits like healthcare, a 401(k) plan, or sick days aren't part of the package. Instead, those "benefits" were paid directly from my business checking account. There was no paid time off or paternity leave. There were times when I longed for the days when my employer would match my retirement contribution or when I could expense travel or meals on the corporate account. On a side note, I find it laughable when people say that they want to start their own company so they can have more free time. The exact opposite happens when you start a business.

Anyway, based on where I was as a business owner in 2016, if I had reported directly to a boss or a board of directors, they wouldn't have rehired me. They would've immediately given me a pink slip with no severance. In turn, I would've sued Legal-Zoom for letting an amateur like me start a business.

In short, I was a not-so-new business owner who wasn't paying as close attention to cash flow or financial statements as I should've been. I wasn't putting in the required effort to generate more business. And truth be told, I had stopped learning.

It's hard to admit now, but at times, I was naïve about what it meant to be a solopreneur who had to manage all facets of business: sales, marketing, accounting, travel, and more. Some-times I waited for business to come my way instead of hunting for it. I paid more attention to my social media likes than to my balance sheet. (It turns out likes, hearts, retweets, and views don't pay the bills.) I even invested in online courses that I thought would provide shortcuts and hacks.

Yeah, as I looked at my last thirty days, I wouldn't have re-hired me.

Now, let's start with you and your work, whether you go to an office every day or run your own business. If this doesn't exactly match where you are in your life right now, get creative (for example, if you're current a student, think about your time in the classroom).

Based on your last thirty days of work, if your company had to decide whether or not to rehire you, would they?

Before you answer, think back to when you got hired for your current job or started your company or endeavor. Remem-ber how nervous you were during the interview process or in those early days?

How about that feeling of excitement that pulsed through your body when you got the call that you'd landed the job or when the paperwork was complete? Can you remember how fired up you were during the first week on the job and even those first few months?

Now ask yourself: "How much of that person still exists? Is he or she still there? Would your company rehire you?" Here are five metrics to help you assess if they would.

Has "good enough" replaced great? Do you ever go above and beyond on projects, or do you stop at just "good enough"?

Does getting promoted seem like a burden? Do you balk at the idea of taking on new challenges because you're too comfortable and fear shaking things up?

Have you stopped building relationships? Have you noticed that people stopped inviting you to lunch, happy hours, or outings because you always decline?

Did you stop taking action on your ideas? When you get new ideas, do you act on them or do you let them gather dust in a notebook or on a hard drive?

Have you stopped learning? Do you get excited about developing new skills, or are you checked out to the point where you don't feel as sharp as you once did?

Imagine if you started your job with the experience you have today. Imagine the opportunities you could take advantage of, and the powerful difference you could make. This isn't a hypothetical, this is your present-day situation. You can do all of the above right now.

Honestly evaluate your past thirty days of work with the exercises at the end of this chapter. Where do you stand?

RELATIONSHIPS

There are far too many thirty-day spans to count since my wife and I got married in 2015 where she probably wouldn't recommit to me, but detailing my shortcomings on this front is for a different book—one that I need her permission to write. But here are a few.

As a speaker, at times I've traveled anywhere between 7,500 and 10,000 miles a month. There were times when I was on the road for days at a time while my wife was home alone with our twins. Sure, I could rationalize that I was providing for our family. But if on day six of a business trip—when I was literally on the other side of the world facilitating a workshop in India—I had asked myself whether she would immediately recommit to me, I wouldn't have bet in my favor.

Oddly, for a man who can easily speak in front of five thousand people or walk into a room full of strangers and quickly make friends, at home I can be quiet and reflective. The extrovert my wife saw in public was a stark contrast to the introverted, please-give-me-some-space-so-I-can-recharge husband that she often experienced at home. Years ago, a girlfriend told me in the gentlest way, "I wish you could give me half the energy you give to strangers." I could picture my wife saying this, too. It's sad how we can feel so comfortable giving the people who are closet to us our worst.

Today, it's far too easy to think about the various times in my marriage when my wife and I needed to connect and be on the same team, but instead my actions, or lack thereof, disconnected us. There comes a point when you either must quit or recommit.

Now, let's stop judging me and instead start digging into your personal life. Whether you're married, in a committed relationship, or hoping to be in either in the future, let's put your relationship to the thirty-day test. (If you're currently single, think about past relationships as you answer this.)

Based on your last thirty days of marriage (or whatever relationship you're in), would your partner immediately recommit to you?

Think back to when you first met your partner. Think about all of the things you did to make yourself stand out to look special—special enough that they wanted to go on a date with you.

Think about your first date. How did you act? The way you talked to them. The interest you showed. How you prepared and dressed. Where did you take them? What did you talk about?

Think about all the unique things about that person. Their personality, their quirks, the way they look, and the stories that made you smile, laugh, and eventually come to love them.

Think about your first vacation together—all of the planning leading up to it, then the experience, the joy, of being away with your lover for the first time and how you fell more deeply in love.

If you're married, think about the day you decided to ask this person to marry you (or when you were asked)—and the immediate answer was yes. Think about your wedding day, whether it was a big event, a destination wedding, or quietly held with a justice of the peace. Think about your vows. Do you remember them?

As you remember the origins of your relationship, how much of this person still exists? Are you the same, or not even 50 percent of the person who you once were? Are you still as kind, loving, supportive, open, giving, interested, honest, and trusting as you once were? Or have these attributes been replaced with the indifference of going through the motions?

Honestly evaluate the past thirty days of your relationship with the exercise at the end of this chapter. Where do you stand?

PARENTING

Evaluating my relationship with my kids hurts at times. As I write this, they are toddlers, and based on what they've experienced up to this point in their lives over thirty-day spans, would they immediately want me as their father?

Primarily raised by a single mother, I've been on a search to learn what it means to be a man my whole life. This journey began anew when I became the father of twins in 2016.

After their births, I didn't feel a deep connection initially, but rather a disconnection. *What does a dad do?* The question of what it really means to be a father played on repeat in my mind. Before my parents were divorced, my own father drank far too much and at times abused my mother. I knew I didn't want to repeat that kind of behavior. But what kind of father *did* I want to be?

As infants, my kids would wake up crying in the middle of the night, needing a diaper change or a warm bottle. If they knew how many times I pretended to be fast asleep, forcing my exhausted wife to get up instead, would they still want me as their father?

When instead of reading them a book, I chose to watch a random NBA basketball game on my tablet, would they still want me as their father? Or, when I did read them books, if they knew that I'd occasionally read a CliffsNotes version to get through it faster, would they still want me as their dad?

When they wanted to be picked up and I constantly said, "Just a minute," while I checked work e-mail, it doesn't put the odds in my favor that they'd want me as their dad.

Now, if you have children, let's put your parenting to the thirty-day test.

Based on your last thirty days as a parent (if you're a parent), would your children want you to continue to be their parent?

Think back to when you first realized that you wanted to have kids or learned that you were going to be a parent. What did you feel inside? Maybe it was excitement combined with some fear of the unknown.

Think about the excitement that family and friends shared when you told them the great news.

Think back to before your kid was born or adopted and the promises you made to your unborn child about the kind of parent you'd be, the kind of life you'd provide, and how you'd always protect them. How you'd be different and avoid the mistakes that your parents made.

Think about the day your kid was born and you heard their first cry and held their tiny body in your arms, rocking them slowly back and forth.

Think about the day when you checked them out of the hospital and how slow the car ride was as you drove back to your home. Think about all the joy this child has brought to your life.

How much of that man or woman still resides inside of you? Do you still aspire to provide your child with a certain type of life? Are you truly showing up for your kid the way they need you to? Are you present and patient with your children? Do you listen to them? What type of example are you setting?

Being a parent is hard, yet meaningful work. Honestly evaluate the past thirty days of your role as a parent with the exercises at the end of this chapter. Where do you stand?

THE NEXT 30 DAYS

The "last thirty days" questions hold a mirror up to the very things that we generally sweep under the rug. It's time to pull the rug up, because a lot of dirt needs to be exposed and cleaned up.

Cleaning up the dirt is, well, a dirty job. But you can end up with a cleaner floor, or life, if you're willing. I used the word *cleaner* because aiming for "perfect" will only lead to repeated failure—but setting "cleaner" as your bull's-eye will help you see progress.

I'm happy to say that I no longer treat my business like a hobby. The man I now show up as for my wife and kids hardly resembles the one who I was just a few years back. To be clear, I'm nowhere near perfect and will always have room for improvement. However, I feel more grounded than ever in what it means to be a husband and a father.

The difference today is that I regularly acknowledge and confront my faults head-on and take responsibility for keeping my side of the street clean. It's an ongoing process and something that I must recommit to every single day.

I'm guessing this chapter may have been challenging for you, but it's necessary. It's not always easy to ask ourselves these tough questions. Moreover, it's hard to show up every day and do this work—but I promise you it's worth it.

The opportunity we have is to truly understand where we stand in the most important aspects of our lives. This will lay the foundation for bigger changes down the road.

NEXT STEPS

1. Based on your last thirty days of work, if your company had to *decide whether or not* to rehire you, would they? If yes, why? If no, why not?

2. Based on your last thirty days of marriage (or your most important relationship), would this person immediately recommit to you? If yes, why? If no, why not?

3. If you're a parent, based on your last thirty days in this role, would your children want you to continue to be their caregiver? If yes, why? If no, why not?

4. Identify other areas in your life to evaluate, based on the last thirty days. For example, your friendships, physical or mental health, or even personal finances.

3

WHAT'S YOUR STORY?

"Know from whence you came. If you know whence you came, there are absolutely no limitations to where you can go."

—JAMES BALDWIN, NOVELIST AND PLAYWRIGHT

STORIES HOLD POWER. They help us make sense of the world, the complexity of being human, and in the end, what it means to be ourselves.

The stories we tell ourselves about our lives are extremely important. Of course, there'll be parts we're proud of—and some we aren't. But together, they make us who we are. So regardless of how the last thirty days of your life have played out, we're going to dig deeper into the person you've become, the story that's led you here, and what kind of ending you're after.

Our whole lives, sometimes unbeknownst to us, we've been crafting a story about who we are and who we aren't. It's like a book that's never been written down—a narrative that we've told ourselves, and that others have witnessed through our actions or words. It informs our confidence, our self-esteem, our self-love, our expectations, and our compassion for ourselves and others.

Some of the stories we've told ourselves help us stand taller and walk prouder. Other stories that we've heard in our inner monologue can cause us to shrink and retreat in defeat from life.

It's critical that we tell ourselves the *right* story. The right story, or stories, will eventually provide us with a strong foundation to weather any success or adversity. So how do we know which story to tell ourselves?

To use a metaphor from those home improvement TV shows, before we "open up the space" in our lives by tearing down walls, we must first understand which walls are critical to keeping the house standing. Similarly, there are load-bearing stories in our lives—the supporting stories that serve as the foundation for who we are.

One of the toughest things for people to acknowledge is that their story isn't exactly what they thought it would be at this point. When you first dreamed up your story, maybe life wasn't filled with the challenges and hardships you experience today. There was a time when you believed in yourself. You had limitless potential, big dreams, boundless confidence, and high aspirations for yourself. But at some point, you arrived at a train station (a major decision point in your life), got on a fast-moving train, and never asked where it was going.

This is the proverbial train that most of us get on. And before we know it, the train changes tracks—again, and again, and again. Your eventual destination is where you stand today. Maybe where you're standing is amazing. But chances are, if you're reading this book, you're not sure it's the right place for you. Nowhere is this more evident than in the communities that some of us choose to belong to.

Once, I read a Facebook post where a "friend" asked the seemingly simple question: "What's your first thought when you wake up?" More than 130 people commented on the post and some of their responses included: "This again . . ." "F*ck my life . . ." "Ugh . . ." "Not again . . ." "Is it the weekend yet?"

The comments made me sad, because I know firsthand what it's like to wake up with similar thoughts about the day to come and feeling stuck.

At some point along the way, maybe while you were living life and checking off the boxes society asked you to check off, you got stuck in your ways. It's possible that you've become unwilling to change your mind, holding on to what once was, even when encountering new information that says otherwise. The routines that you created for a purpose (though you can't exactly remember what that purpose was) have become a hamster wheel that holds you back from your true potential. Today, you're looking for a way to step off the wheel, find your footing, and take control once again.

Chances are, you've let yourself indulge in your worst self-doubts: Have I passed my prime? Am I in the wrong relationship? Did I miss my big opportunity? Will my kids always be so challenging? Why have I been eating gluten-free food all these years?

When you browse the social media accounts of friends, colleagues, and influencers to distract yourself from life and seek inspiration, you walk away feeling dejected and exhausted. Apparently, everyone is "winning" at life, hustling hard, traveling to exotic locations that you'll never visit, eating five-star meals, and getting into peak physical shape. That is, everyone except you.

Inside, you know it's not fair to compare your "real life" to someone's curated social media highlight reel, yet when you do, your anxiety spikes to an uncomfortable level. You feel as if you've been abandoned and forgotten. More than ever, it's hard to relax and take those deep breaths that serve you all too well. You even think that maybe cigarette smokers know something you don't—because at least they get regular smoke breaks throughout the day, while the rest of us keep slogging away at our desks.

It's important to know that you're not alone when it comes to the angst and anxiety that you feel on a daily basis. In fact, it's estimated that Generalized Anxiety Disorder affects nearly seven million people in the United States, according to the Anxiety and Depression Association of America.[1]

But the good news is, even in the face of anxiety or angst, you're not ready to give up. That's why we're here. You crave that happiness, meaning, and purpose you keep reading about in articles and books. Though you may feel exhausted, you've still got some fuel left in your tank. You're like a high-powered jet barreling down the runway that hasn't taken off—but come hell or high water, you want to get some altitude and feel the wind beneath your wings.

Here's a little secret society doesn't want you to know: even if you've felt like life has been beyond your grasp up until now, you've always been in control of your story. Odds are, you probably have just been on cruise control, following the crowd. Today the opportunity is to focus less on external factors, and more on what we can do internally to find peace with who we've become and where we are before we can move forward. As I heard someone once say:

The world isn't full of victims. It's full of volunteers.

No matter where you stand today, odds are that you greatly undervalue and underestimate your wealth of experience. The fact is that everything that's happened in your life has led you to this moment. Every story, every decision, and every memory shapes who you are now and who you'll choose to become. Your path is uniquely yours. Learning from and embracing your stories that have gotten you here is going to be essential to moving forward. To be blunt with you:

*Your story
is remarkable,
even if you don't
know it yet.*

WHAT YOU CAN LEARN FROM A BAD TATTOO

During my sophomore year of college, some friends and I visited a small tattoo parlor that I remember to be more like someone's dilapidated basement in a run-down neighborhood.

As we exited my 1994 Mercury Topaz, the tattoo artist greeted the four of us. She was squat, had long brown hair, wore impossibly thick glasses, and looked about fifty, even though she was probably in her late thirties. An unlit cigarette hung from her lip.

"Hey fellas," she said, as we entered the "studio" (which was actually a living room). "Pick any tattoo you want," she said, as if we were already customers. Then added, pointing, "The book is over there."

The "book" was actually a photo album. "I can do every tattoo in that book except the dragons," she said. "Dragons hurt my wrist."

On the pages of the photo album were images you would expect to see in the mid-1990s: leopards, tigers, lions, horses, dolphins, swords, lots of stuff with fire, various font types, and yes, dragons.

Something immediately told me that picking a random tattoo from a random photo album in a random tattoo parlor wasn't a good idea. I wasn't a jaguar-on-my-arm kind of guy. Still, like most of the others, I was committed to getting a tattoo thanks to some old-school peer pressure. My dad had plenty of tattoos on his arms and chest from his days in the 82nd Airborne Division of the United States Army. So, I decided that if tattoos were good enough for Mr. Neves, they were definitely good enough for me.

After watching my friends sit in a wicker chair and proudly get tatted, and after going back and forth and stalling, I made the ill-fated decision to get my own name—yes, "Antonio"—tattooed on the top of my left arm.

For the font style, I went to my car and grabbed a CD that I'd been listening to. It was rhythm-and-blues songstress Faith Evans's first album. In the album artwork, she had her name tattooed on her arm in a feminine cursive design that I liked.

When I showed it to the tattoo artist, she raised an eyebrow and showed hesitation for the first time. "You want *that* font? What about Old English?" When I shook my head no, she started poking my skin with what I hoped was a clean needle. She then went on to create one of my best worst mistakes.

Since getting that tattoo more than twenty years ago, here are just a few things that I've heard when my arm isn't covered:

Is that just in case you forget your name?

Is that your boyfriend's name?

Are you getting your social security number next?

What's up with the font, bro?

Or, when about to get down and dirty with women over the years, I would hear some variation of:

Oh my God. Is that your name on your arm? I'm not sure we should do this. What time is it?

By my late twenties, I had reached the point of my tattoo "getting on my last nerve," as Grandma Ella would say. So, I scheduled an appointment with a dermatologist to learn about getting it removed with laser technology.

After a brief assessment (that included asking me why I got my own name tattooed on my body), the dermatologist told me that while it would be extremely painful, over a series of sessions he could remove the tattoo to the point where only I would be able to tell that there used to be a bad tattoo there. This was encouraging news, but something didn't feel right. It felt like the doctor was being super judgmental and treating me like I had a street gang tattoo on my face.

Even with mixed emotions, I remember going home feeling good about scheduling an appointment to get my permanent name badge removed. But something odd happened. After processing this decision for a few days, I changed my mind. I realized that—even though my tattoo was the butt of way too many jokes—it was *my* tattoo. Part of my story. My journey in life. So, I decided to keep it.

Today, my wife doesn't necessarily hate my "Antonio" tattoo, but she giggles when she sees it. My toddler twins have reached the age where they understand that there's something odd about Daddy having his name permanently inked on his body. And, I've come to accept that I'm a grown-ass man with my first name etched on my left deltoid. I've also come to embrace and accept, and no longer regret, the decision to get the tattoo during my college days in the first place.

WHAT HAVE YOU YET TO ACCEPT?

Sometimes the things we are most ashamed of are actually the stories we most need to embrace. Even more, the things that we think make us fragile, weak, and vulnerable can also be the things that have helped us develop grit, resilience, and character. With the right perspective, these can be the experiences that actually give us strength.

Does my bad tattoo give me strength? Well, that may be a stretch. But it does remind me that I have lived. That I made a choice. That I've made decisions, good and bad, and I've learned and rebounded from all of them.

All of our decisions in life play a similar role. We may not like them. Maybe we even regret them. But every single one has a story to tell and a lesson to teach.

It's important to remember that we're not here to judge ourselves or question our past decisions. Instead, we're here to get curious. We're here to wonder. We're here to go "Hmmm" instead of "Hmph!" We're here to take full accountability and responsibility for our lives and decisions.

Regardless of that boss who passed you over for that promotion, or that person you were madly in love with who broke up with you on Valentine's Day, that business partner who screwed you over and left you in debt, or those parents who made far too many mistakes, this is where you stand today. What you've experienced in your life may not be your fault but moving forward from these experiences is your job and no one else's.

So, before we can go any further, there's one thing you absolutely must do.

You must accept where you are today in your life as an adult without excuses or blame.

I write that we must accept where we are as an *adult* because it's easy for us to revert to behaving like a child, based on the whims of our emotions. This is where we point fingers and take little to no responsibility for our lives. Being a true adult means living based not solely on emotions (they'll eventually pass), but instead based on standards and values. This is when we point a loving finger at ourselves and take full accountability.

It's only once we accept where we are that we can begin to make progress: "Here is where I am. Whether I like it or not, in some shape or form, I have participated in creating my circumstances by the choices I have or haven't made."

This probably stings some, right? Like pouring rubbing alcohol on a cut. Doing this sure as hell isn't easy. If everyone were willing to do it, we wouldn't recognize life on this planet. Holiday get-togethers with family would be totally different! But hopefully, this wakes you up and gets you to start taking action. Again: *What part of your story or journey in life do you still need to accept?*

Maybe it's a bad tattoo, like mine. A relationship that came to an end. A job, or jobs, that didn't end up as you hoped. Something your parents did (or didn't do). An investment you made that went awry. The options abound.

What's the thing that if you said it out loud to someone, you'd be afraid of or embarrassed by their reaction? Whatever it is, I ask you to start to own it. Hell, to actually love it. To forgive what needs to be forgiven, whether it's forgiving yourself or others. When you have the courage to do this, it actually frees up the necessary space you need to live a better story. It's like cleaning out the house of a hoarder. Finally, there's space to move around, think, and just be. And you might just find what you've been missing all along.

GET OUT OF THE PAST TENSE

If you'd like an indicator of what some people have yet to own, just take a look at social media bios these days. Instead of bios that identify what people want or what their future holds, you'll see bios that include words like *former* or *past* followed by things they've done, places they've worked, or schools they've attended. All past tense. Rarely is there anything that's forward-looking. I know this all too well.

When I first transitioned to leadership and development work, it was hard for me to accept that my past career in the so-called glamorous television industry was over. When introducing myself to new people, it was like I had something to prove. Instead of saying "I'm a leadership and development speaker, trainer, and executive coach," I'd begin by saying, "I worked in the TV industry in New York City for more than ten years with networks like NBC, PBS, Nickelodeon . . ." in an attempt to prove to others that I had value. It's taken me years to accept the following:

> *Your past doesn't determine your future.*
> *What matters is what you're going to do with those*
> *past experiences to start moving forward.*

If we look at life through the right lens, living is actually a way of gathering data—of establishing a track record and gaining experience by making decisions. And this is where responsibility and accountability come from—not being a person who shies away or hides from owning your past.

Did I get a bad tattoo when I was nineteen? I sure did. Would I do it again today? Hell to the no. But it's my story and it's an interesting one to tell. And as I was once told:

Live an interesting life. No one wants to talk to an old person who doesn't have interesting stories to tell. No stories means never having lived.

Right now, there are many people who've just sat in the corner their whole lives, avoiding making any real decisions. They've been in default mode. They judge others. At the end of the day, they're just projecting their own lack of decision making and ownership in their lives. But hey, that's not you—at least, it doesn't have to be. Making choices is fundamental to living the authentic, exciting life you crave.

Let me ask you this: When was the last time you made a

decision that you may end up regretting? Or to reframe that as a positive, when was the last time you made a decision that you might end up thanking yourself for later? Think about some of the mistakes you made or decisions you regret that you'd like to let go of (or accept). What are some of the lessons that you learned from these stories?

Don't be afraid to make decisions because of how the world might see you. Instead, be afraid not to make decisions based on how *you* might see you.

LIFE ISN'T LIVED ONLINE

When I deliver speeches at corporations, conferences, or universities, I typically use about fifteen PowerPoint slides for a one-hour talk. The slides vary from powerful imagery to key takeaways that I want the audience to remember.

After delivering hundreds of these talks, there's one slide that consistently stands out as the most powerful. Is it the slide with the mountain peak paired with the intentionally lame inspirational quote I use to make fun of myself as a motivational speaker? No, although that's a good one. The most memorable slide has absolutely nothing on it. It's blank.

Here's how it works. At the beginning of my talks, I like to provide some context for the audience about the guy on the stage talking into a microphone to establish some trust. I share a bit about my professional background to help audiences learn about me. To do this, I show them what they'd find if they did a Google search of my name.

On a slide, I display all the logos of the television networks I worked with like Nickelodeon, NBC, PBS, and BET; the covers of my books; the media outlets that I've written for, like

Inc.com and *Entrepreneur.com*; and for good measure, I also share a photo of my early days cohosting that children's television show on Nickelodeon.

Then I share that my intention with the slide isn't to brag or to boast, but rather to show what a Google search of my name turns up—and to make the important point that the Internet doesn't tell the whole story. Not even close.

What we see in Google search results can be extremely misleading. That's because when we Google ourselves, or someone else, what we're seeing is what others *want* us to see. With social media, personal websites, and more, we tend to craft and share stories with the intention to impress and make others say, "Wow." Please know:

Though we may impress by sharing the best versions of ourselves, it's only with sharing authentic stories that we truly can connect as human beings with others.

The truth is, the things that make you special, the things that make you unique, and the things that make you stand out, rarely, if ever, show up on a Google search.

Though I'm not ashamed of what a Google search of my name generates, the results will not tell you about my tattoo. Nor will a Google search reveal anything about who I really am and what my lifelong journey to get to where I am today really looks like—which, in a sense, is the *real* story. The one that makes people lean in and want to learn more.

Now, back to that completely blank slide that I share in presentations. That's where I tell the audience the story that Google could never tell.

I share that I was raised in a small town in Michigan, not far from a NASCAR speedway.

I share that my hometown is one of those places where it

seemed like people never left. At one time, they didn't have to leave. Good-paying factory jobs that supported the automobile industry were always available if you knew the right person and weren't afraid of some hard work. As for me, I couldn't wait to leave.

I share that as a child, I experienced what you might call a significant amount of instability. Or to reframe it in terms of personal-development speak, I had an upbringing that cultivated "grit," "resilience," and "character."

I share that between my mother and father are a total of six divorces and that before I graduated high school, I had moved more than ten times within my small hometown.

I share that I lived briefly in a shelter for victims of domestic abuse.

I also share that growing up, there were times I remember feeling poor, even though we were never completely broke, and at times we lived in nice, middle-class neighborhoods. Still, leaving my hometown was my way out.

My intention with sharing this with the audience isn't to make anyone feel sorry for me. Instead, it's to build connection and trust. It's to reinforce the point that Google can never tell anyone's whole story—at least the parts that really matter.

What I've found is that when I share these stories, the audience really feels like they know me. I've become not just the speaker from out of town on the stage under the bright lights, but rather a human being who has lived life just like them.

LIFE ON PAPER

Of the thousands of college students I've met over the years at speaking events across the United States, a few truly stand out of the crowd. It's not their résumés that make them impressive, but rather the little details that so many people overlook. One student who comes to mind is a young man I met at an event in Philadelphia.

After I delivered a speech, he confidently came up and introduced himself. During our conversation, he shared that he had researched my background and knew that I'd worked in television. Then he shared his goal of getting an internship at a local news TV station and asked if he could schedule some time to talk with me about it.

A few weeks later, he e-mailed me. And even though I didn't initially respond, he followed up again. He wasn't pushy—instead, he showed a kind persistence and we eventually had a great phone call, during which I answered as many of his questions as I could about breaking into television.

Months later, when I found myself back in Philadelphia for another speaking engagement, I met up with him for coffee. He excitedly shared the good news that he'd landed that coveted internship at the local station. Then he said something that got my attention. "The recruiter said that *on paper,* I wasn't her first choice," he admitted. "But I won her over in the job interview."

"On paper" is the equivalent of a Google search. "How did you win her over?" I asked.

"I prepared like crazy for that job interview," he said. "I knew everything about the television station, industry trends, and her background. I asked great questions. And like you suggested, I shared those important things about me that would never appear on a résumé. The interview was supposed to be thirty minutes, but it lasted two hours!"

After the student and I parted ways, I couldn't shake what he said: "On paper" he wasn't her first choice. The truth is that there aren't really any metrics for grit, resilience, or persistence—or sharing your true story. We must look beyond what's "on paper"—in ourselves, and in others.

WHAT MAKES YOU, YOU

As it turns out, many of the things that would never show up on a Google search or "on paper"—things we've possibly tried to hide over the years—can actually be our superpowers.

What we find boring or normal about ourselves, others may find fascinating.

Over the years, when I've facilitated workshops across the country and around the globe, people have shared some of the things a Google search would never reveal about them—and it blows me away every single time.

People have shared how Google won't tell you they work a full-time job during the week and drive for Uber on the evenings and weekends to help pay for their kids' education. One woman shared how when she lost her grandmother to pancreatic cancer, she started dedicating her time to raising thousands of dollars to find a cure for this terrible disease. Another woman shared how she regularly takes in foster children and adopts them because she once was part of the state system and doesn't want anyone to experience what she did. And one gentleman shared how he volunteers his time with his church every year to teach English to children in a developing country.

From a career perspective, and with clients that I've coached, I've discovered that finding organic ways to share these types of experiences in job interviews helps people stand out and be memorable.

What we're talking about are the profound experiences that shaped us and got us to where we are today—even with all of our scars, visible or invisible. It doesn't matter what story Google, a piece of paper, or the rest of the Internet tells. What really matters is the story you tell yourself. And if you don't like the story you're hearing, it's time to remedy that.

Remember that exercise in the first chapter where you listed the five best things to happen in your life, not including the traditional societal markers of success? Take a moment to look at it again. What would you add to the list now? What are the things that have helped shape and mold you into the amazing person you are today?

NEXT STEPS

1. Write down three to five "mistakes" you made or decisions you regret that you'd like to let go of—or rather, accept as part of your story.

2. For each of those "mistakes" or decisions, write down a possible lesson or story that you can take away from that experience.

3. Write down five things about you that make you special that would never show up on a Google search. What about these five things make your story unique?

4. How would you introduce yourself to a group of strangers if you couldn't reference your job or career path? What stories would you tell?

4

WOULD YOU BET ON YOU?

"A destiny is not something that awaits us, it is something we have to achieve in the midst of innumerable circumstantial impediments and detours."

—GEOFF DYER, *OUT OF SHEER RAGE*

AS WE ESTABLISHED, part of becoming a person—of living—is making decisions, accepting our mistakes, learning lessons along the way, and harnessing those hard-won lessons into the story of who we are. Still, how do we determine who we want to be? How can we examine our most recent day-to-day experiences to help guide our path forward?

To do this, we have to get something out of the way. Brace yourself. *You are going to die.*

Technically, we all know this, but somehow we can delude ourselves into thinking, *This whole death thing isn't going to happen to me.*

Now look, I know that our eventual demise maybe isn't the most cheerful way of looking forward. But the truth is, you can drink as much green juice as you like, eat gluten-free food, attempt to freeze off your excess body fat in a chamber, or do CrossFit, and still, all of us share the same final destination. Our party on this planet isn't forever.

We're going to explore something that may seem morbid,

but it's actually designed to help you feel more *alive* than ever. To ensure that your best days are ahead of you, the first step is to actually consider how much of your life you have left to live and what's at stake.

This activity first hit me a few years back while I was reading an obituary, a random hobby of mine. What's fascinating about obituaries is that in just a short paragraph or two, you can learn so much about someone's *life*—how they lived, what they stood for, and the legacy, or lack thereof, that they're leaving behind.

After reading a brilliant obituary, the first question that always comes to my mind is, "Would I have wanted to know this person?" The next questions that present themselves are:

What will my obituary say when I'm gone?

What did I truly care about and stand for?

How did I make a difference?

What legacy did I leave behind?

Who's reading my journals and going through all my personal stuff?

Obituaries are a great reminder that, no matter how much we do to complicate life, it's actually painfully simple. When we're born, we're given an extremely straightforward user manual that the vast majority of us tend to ignore. This manual essentially says:

Step 1: Congratulations! Your parents had unprotected sex, or you were created in a laboratory with the help of scientists. Welcome to planet Earth! Now it's time to start living. Your journey has begun.

Step 2: Just so you're aware, one day you're going to die. You'll no longer exist on this planet that's spinning at roughly *one thousand miles per hour in space. The journey will come to an end.*

Step 3: *Just for fun, and to add an element of mystery, we're not going to tell you when Step 2 is going to happen.*

Whoever wrote Step 3 has a dark sense of humor, right? I mean, come on. You can't even give me an idea of when it'll all end? Not even a five- or three-year window? Not cool.

Now, I would add a fourth step to the manual.

Step 4: *No matter the length of time, what you do in between being born and dying is called living.*

THE DASH

To bring this celebration of death to life, let's do a simple exercise.

First, write down the year that you were born on a piece of paper. For example: 1980.

Now, write down a dash after the year like this: 1980–

Then, add eighty to the year that you were born and put it after the dash like this:

1980–2060

What you see on that piece of paper or screen in front of you is roughly the average life span of someone existing in the United States. I write *existing* because that's what most are doing, simply existing instead of *living*.

Sure, you may live longer. Or, you may kick the bucket sooner. Regardless, this makes things crystal clear. You are going to die. Now you have a rough idea of when that could happen.

How does seeing what could be your life span make you feel? Anxious? Fearful? Do you want to take shots of tequila?

1980–2060

The time we live is the dash, that short dash, between when we're born and when we die.

My hope is that after taking a few deep breaths, seeing these dates in black and white will provide you with more clarity and acceptance that your ride isn't forever. That it'll serve as a reminder to start living a life worth living. To be clear, I'm not suggesting that you file for divorce, quit your job, cash in your money market account, sell all of your belongings, and backpack around the world. Life can indeed be long. What I am saying is that what we do with *today*—our time, our energy, our focus, and our choices—matters more than anything else.

THE DICE ARE IN YOUR HANDS— THEY ALWAYS HAVE BEEN

Now that you've had a chance to get super real with yourself and actually consider when you may stop breathing, let's gamble with another idea.

Imagine that you're in one of my least favorite cities on the planet, Las Vegas.

You're walking down the Vegas strip, surrounded by tons of people. You take in all the bright lights, sights, sounds, and not-so-great smells.

You see the street performers dressed in ill-fitting superhero costumes. A person dances around dressed as a dingy Sponge-Bob SquarePants. There are G-string sightings galore, exposed above low-cut jeans with bedazzled back pockets.

Drunk people dance in the street, drinking Hurricanes in

those super-long plastic souvenir cups they paid extra for, but won't be able to fit in their suitcases when it's time to hit the airport—hungover, inebriated, or both.

As you take in the visual chaos, you get distracted by the bright flashing lights of the many casinos advertising the opportunity to "Win big!" To escape the madness of the strip, you decide to head inside one of those massive, Walmart-sized casinos.

When you walk in, it's like you've been transported into another universe. There's not a clock to be found and the beige and maroon carpet could mask even the most disgusting vomit. You observe chain-smoking octogenarians in wheelchairs and so many dudes in tank tops, wearing their baseball caps backward.

Who are these people? you think. Bored servers clad in short skirts and halter tops power walk through the vast casino and serve "free" watered-down Jack and Cokes for dismal tips.

You decide to head to the back of the casino, where people are betting on sporting events. The Sportsbook. You look up at a giant digital video screen and see a long list of all the options: basketball, boxing, horse racing, dog racing, soccer, golf, cricket, you name it. You can even bet on people playing video games or e-sports.

Listed next to each sporting event are the odds for who's going to win the event and how much you can win if you bet on them.

As you observe the odds for a cricket match happening in India, something grabs your attention. You stand up straighter. You get butterflies in your stomach, your heart rate increases. Among all the games and events that you can bet on, you notice *your* name.

People are betting on *you.*

People are betting on whether you'll accomplish what you

say is most important in this life. You start to sweat, your hands start to tremble, and your throat goes dry.

The idea of people betting on you makes you feel really uncomfortable—kind of like when you have to urinate during a long drive, but you know there won't be a rest stop with a bathroom for another thirty minutes. Still, you get curious and wonder if the odds are in your favor or against you.

If you were a betting woman or man, would you bet on you? You hesitate. Just then, out of the corner of your eye, you see a dear family member heading toward the stall to place a bet. They're about to bet their life savings on *you* doing all that it takes to make your dreams come true. You start to panic.

Would you let them bet on you? Or would you immediately rush over to stop them from losing all of their money?

The question now begs:

Are the odds in your favor at "winning" at life, or are they against you?

To determine your odds, all you have to do is look back over your last thirty days.

What would it take for you to willingly bet everything on you? To allow others to bet everything on you, knowing that whether you win or lose, you gave *everything*. Do you even know what everything is?

What we're talking about is an investment rather than a sacrifice.

LAS VEGAS IS YOUR LIFE

In more ways than one, life is like a Las Vegas casino.

Whether you know it or not, every single day you're betting everything on yourself with the effort you do (or don't) put forward. Instead of gambling with our money, we instead routinely gamble with our lives—based on the decisions we make (or don't make). Believe it or not, we aren't the only ones betting on ourselves.

Our parents bet on us when they raise us and pay for our college educations.

Our spouses bet on us to always be there for them in good times and in bad.

Our children bet on us to take care of them every day.

Companies that hire us bet on us to be productive and engaged employees.

Even institutions like banks or credit card companies bet on us to meet our obligations every month (while they simultaneously take advantage of us).

Hell, even our friends bet on us to help them move apartments, take them to the airport at 5:00 a.m., or be there for them even as life takes twists and turns.

So, are you gambling away your life or making every moment count? Based on your past actions, are you living a life you'll be proud of or one that'll be filled with regrets?

More importantly, can others reliably bet on you? What we're talking about is trust. Trust is earned. When it comes to betting, here's another thing I learned:

If you don't bet on yourself, no one else will.

TAKING A "RISK"

As you may recall, I had that less-than-inspiring stint in a perfectly good job selling cheese for a living in south Florida. Well, after less than a year of selling cheese, I could no longer take the upset stomachs of dread on Monday mornings before I began the workweek. (Maybe this feeling of dread is why some studies[1] find that heart attack rates rise on Monday mornings.)

The constant "What if . . ." scenarios playing in my mind became exhausting. The "What if there's more than this?" question played nonstop on a loop in my brain. Every single day, the metaphorical taps I felt on my shoulder kept repeating, *This isn't what you're supposed to be doing with your life.*

Plus, it probably didn't help that my girlfriend at the time had just broken up with me via fax. The guy at Kinko's knew my relationship was over before I did. It was starting to feel like I had more to lose by *not* making a change in my life.

When the pain of staying is greater than the pain of leaving, you know it's time to make a change.

So, I took what seemed like the biggest risk ever. Against the wishes of family and friends, I quit my job selling cheese. I packed up a U-Haul truck and moved to New York City. All I had was about eight hundred dollars in my checking account and a dream. I didn't know it then, but that was all I needed. It doesn't matter how much is in your bank account or who you do or don't know. What matters is what's in your heart—and your willingness to act on it.

At the time, I had never been to New York City. There wasn't a job waiting for me. And I only knew one person who lived there. I moved anyway. Although I didn't know it at the time, I was placing the first big bet on myself.

Betting on yourself means being willing to do something uncomfortable for the greater good even when everything, or everyone, says not to.

The greater good is a feeling deep inside you. It's knowing that more is being asked of you, or that something else is out there that you're being called to experience and live. In many ways, this *greater good* is like our compass directing us in the right direction—if we're willing to pay attention to the coordinates it provides.

Betting on yourself is the moment when you choose to go for broke, not knowing if everything will work out. But you know that what you've been doing *isn't* working out.

Betting on yourself is how you end up with an obituary that others will read and say, "I wish I knew them." The people who did know you will be glad they did.

Almost *three years* after I arrived in New York City, I caught my first big break. My family and friends back in Michigan, even the ones who told me I was crazy for leaving my job selling cheese and that Ford Taurus, could turn on their television sets and watch me every weekday on television.

This is a testament, a reminder, that *if you won't bet on you, no one else will.*

A NOTE ON FEAR

Yes, betting on yourself can be absolutely scary. But it's important for us to remember that fear can be twofold. It can be a sign that we're pushing ourselves to try new things, expand our boundaries of what we think is possible. That's good fear. Conversely, there can also be the kind of fear that holds us back from living our lives and spreading our wings. Here's a great way to think about it:

Bad fear keeps us standing still.
Good fear propels us forward.

We all have fears that hold us back. As much as we try to hide them, they confront us every day when we look in the mirror. Some fear getting a terminal sickness. Others fear losing a loved one. And some fear going bankrupt and losing everything.

When I share one of my greatest fears, people are often surprised. As briefly mentioned in the introduction of this book, my fear is that one day I'll bump into someone I knew years ago and they'll look at me and say, "What happened to you?"

What they'd be asking is, "What happened to the person back then who was full of optimism, vigor, and unleashed potential? There was nothing he wasn't going to do. There was no leaf he would leave unturned. There was nowhere he wasn't going to visit. When did he stop betting on himself?"

These days, I don't fear that question as much anymore. I confront it head-on. Because what I fear more than someone asking me that question is letting life go by without holding myself accountable.

I've experienced both good fear and bad fear in my life—and they've both reminded me that although my life isn't perfect, it's unrealistic to expect that it will be. Still, I continue to make progress even amid periodic setbacks. I do my best to tackle my fears little by little, day by day. Because at the end of the day, this is the only way to make the most of that time between when we're born and when we die.

DON'T WAIT FOR A NEAR-DEATH EXPERIENCE

In late 2019, when I experienced turbulence like never before and smelled fumes in the air on a flight from North Carolina to Virginia, I immediately knew that something was wrong.

The fact that we had had multiple delays due to "maintenance issues" prior to takeoff didn't help my confidence. I really knew things weren't right when I looked at the flight attendant.

Flight attendants' demeanors have always been my indicator of whether things were going to be okay, or if they were about to go in a not-so-fun direction. When I saw the panic in the flight attendant's eyes and she reached for a manual that I'd never seen anyone reach for before, it was crystal clear that this wasn't a drill. It was realer than almost anything I've ever felt before in my life. In that moment, I realized that my obituary exercise was far too generous and that I may not have much more time left.

When the pilot announced that we would "attempt" an emergency landing, and when the flight attendant then read safety instructions about how to properly brace with a quivering voice, all I could think was, *I have two text messages to send.*

The first text went to my mother, saying thank-you for all she did for me, and also asking her to tell my siblings that I love them. The second text I sent, more challenging than the first, was to my wife. It said:

> *"Flight not going as planned. We're gonna do an emergency landing in Raleigh. It's gonna be okay. If anything happens, I love you and the kids with everything. Let the kids know Daddy is always with them. They are Neves strong. Let them know to live a life of discipline, joy, and love. Love you."*

After we were low enough for me to get reception and I saw the bars appear on my phone, I pressed Send. This was the hardest and easiest message I had ever written. After seeing that the messages were sent, I took a deep breath and said quietly,

"Thank you," as I gathered and steadied myself. This was followed by an awkward chuckle, and then I said to myself, "Ain't this some shit?"

Spoiler alert: We landed safely, though aggressively, surrounded by firetrucks and ambulances. But this experience shook me to my core. Ironically, when we landed, I looked over to see someone just waking up, completely unaware of everything that had just taken place. To this day, I'm thankful that I was awake and fully present during this life-changing experience.

My takeaway from all this is that when you're faced with what might be the end of your life, only the important things come to mind. It's a powerful reminder:

Don't wait for a life-altering event to start living the life you're meant to live.

Sadly, that's what most of us are doing with our lives. Waiting. For a sign. For someone else to make a decision. For that winning lottery ticket.

Waiting is like slowly pouring water on a blazing fire. It's still going, but with each passing moment, the fire gets smaller and smaller. The fire I'm talking about is your drive, your passion, and your desire for change.

We've all heard the stories of someone surviving a terrible car accident that should've killed them, beating a fatal disease like cancer, or losing a loved one. It was in those moments of excruciating life-changing pain that they decided to make an intentional shift with their lives.

How would your life change if you experienced a near-death experience? Odds are you would easily be able to finish the following statements:

I would no longer do this . . .

I wouldn't worry about that . . .

I would say what I really want to say . . .

I would travel here . . .

I would spend more time with . . .

I would ignore this . . .

I would tell the people I love most how much they mean to me . . .

I wouldn't get hung up on what doesn't really matter . . .

I would pee outside more often just because . . .

I wouldn't waste time on this . . .

I would finally finish that project I've been talking about . . .

I would . . .

Again, how would your life change if you experienced a near-death experience? Based on your answers, a second question is: What are you waiting for?

The answers to powerful questions like these aren't always easy, but they are necessary. In short, it's worth it. Don't wait.

Always remember, and when in doubt:

You are the
life-altering
event your life
is waiting for.

NEXT STEPS

1. When you do the obituary exercise mentioned at the beginning of this chapter, how does seeing your possible life span written out make you feel? Describe your emotions.

2. Would you bet on you? Based on your track record, would the odds be in your favor or against you when it comes to accomplishing your goals?

3. Make a list of times that you bet on yourself.

4. How would your life change if you experienced a near-death experience? What would you do differently from what you're doing now?

BETTER AND BOLDER

"To feel ambition and to act upon it is to embrace the unique calling of our souls. Not to act upon that ambition is to turn our backs on ourselves and on the reason for our existence."

—STEVEN PRESSFIELD, TURNING PRO

IN A 2016 interview[1] in the *New York Times*, the founders of a popular streetwear label were discussing the ups and downs throughout their lives and careers.

When reminiscing about growing up in New York City, one of the cofounders said, "I miss the old New York."

His cofounder corrected him. "No, you don't," he said. "You miss the old you."

Can you relate? Do you miss the *old* you?

THE OLD YOU

How often have you found yourself reminiscing about the past and the days gone by? Have you ever caught yourself talking to friends or family, saying:

I miss the old days . . .

I miss my old job . . .

I miss the old neighborhood . . .

I miss my ex . . .

I miss college . . .

I miss hooking up with strangers . . .

What I've come to learn over the years is that when we reminisce about the old days, what we're really saying is that we miss who we once were before life got the best of us. What we crave are the emotions and energy we experienced during that time of life.

Chances are, you've heard the criticism about Millennials. According to the media and seemingly everyone older than fifty, Millennials are privileged, cocky, entitled, lazy, impatient, and so much more. In fact, Millennials may be the most hated generation ever.

Why are they the most hated generation ever? The real reason that older generations, like Gen Xers and Baby Boomers, despise Millennials is simple:

Younger generations remind older generations of who they once were.

In short, Millennials are younger and bolder. This resistance to a younger generation isn't new. If anything, it's recycled. This can also be said for people from pretty much every generation that's younger than you. We'll likely be having this same discussion about Gen Zers in just a few years.

Watching others live life the way we once did can stir up nostalgia, unresolved resentment, and disappointment. Whether we know it or not, this can be toxic to our lives and careers.

Let me give you an example. I once had a conversation with a successful fashion designer. On all fronts—from his bank account to his social media profiles to his celebrity network—you'd think this forty-something designer had it all figured out.

However, when I asked him what the twenty-four-year-old version of himself would think of who he had become, he paused before saying, "The twenty-four-year-old me would say that I'm better today than I've ever been before in my life. However, he would also say that I was *bolder* back then."

What's evident is that even though we are better equipped, smarter, and wiser than ever before to deal with life's unexpected turns, for many of us, that boldness has been replaced with passivity.

Maybe this lack of boldness stems from all of the responsibilities we've accumulated over the years. This includes our careers, home lives, finances, and even caring for elderly family members. But the resentment starts to build when we look at our current lives and realize that though we may have impressive résumés, bank accounts, or the latest iPhone, we're not doing what we originally set out to do.

In chapter 1, you did an exercise that identified the emotions you were feeling when you were experiencing the best things that weren't traditional markers of success. Those emotions that you identified are typically what living bolder and better feels and looks like.

If you're not as bold as you once were, and odds are you're not, think about when you stopped being bold. For some, this might've begun when you followed the college major or career path your parents chose for you. For others, it could be that hobby or side hustle that you gave up on because someone told you it was time to be an "adult" and enter the "real world" or get a "real job." It could be when you stopped hanging out with your friends after you got into that relationship. Or, maybe your dream was to travel the world, but you haven't earned a stamp in your passport for far too long.

It begs the question:

When did you stop being bold in your pursuits?

Even if you don't have concrete answers, perhaps you can remember a path or journey at some point in your life that you wanted to pursue, but that you gave up on? Do you feel like you settled for less than what you wanted to achieve?

What I've come to find personally, as well as from working with clients over the years, is that when we hold back our aspirations and don't release them into the world, this can begin to manifest itself in subtle yet destructive ways. It can present as sedating ourselves with food, television, substances, or even the wrong people and the wrong places. What's true is that life is inviting you to start thinking boldly once again.

When we stop being bold, we stop living.

IF YOUR LIFE WAS A MOVIE

A great way to look at your life is to compare it to a movie. A fantastic question to ask (but one that may be hard to answer) is:

If your life up to this point was a movie, would you go see it?

Many people I know and have met over the years would pass on seeing their own life on the big screen. Some people I've asked this question to said that if they ever saw a movie based on their own life, they would walk out of it before it finished. It would put them to sleep. A movie critic would say it's too boring, slow, cliché, or predictable. Based on what I was experiencing in my life in 2016, I would've walked out of my "movie" and immediately requested a refund.

Now, here's another question that's a bit more enjoyable to answer:

If your life was a movie, and the movie was halfway over, what would the lead character start doing to turn things around?

It's a powerful question, if you allow yourself to explore it. Think about this question in the spirit of one of those choose-your-own-adventure books you read during your childhood.

The truth—and I'm sure it's one you agree with—is that we all have the capacity to improve our lives. Starting today. We also all have the power to do the exact opposite: to make decisions that will continue to compromise our lives. Never forget, each of us is just one bad decision away from going to prison.

If you're stuck on what your lead character would start doing right now to turn things around, here are a few choose-your-own-adventure options:

Option A: Keep doing exactly what you're doing. The status quo. The same as yesterday. If you do this, where will you end up a year from now?

Option B: Make decisions that are worse than what you're making right now. You know, develop a drug addiction, get a face tattoo, or cheat on your partner. If you do this, where will you end up a year from now?

Option C: Do something bold and courageous each day, no matter how small it is. If you do this, where will you end up a year from now?

Newsflash: you're the lead character in this movie. What's the best plot twist that will lead to an amazing second act and make the audience lean forward with anticipation? What movie would you and others, like your family and friends, pay for and stay in the theater to see? You know, the kind of film where you stand up and clap at the end—and want to watch over and over.

YOUR DREAMS HAVE AN EXPIRATION DATE

Of course, life isn't a movie. So, I'm going to be straight with you because you deserve to hear the truth. I'm telling you what no pastor, life coach, Instagram influencer, or anyone else who wants your money will. The truth is:

> *Your dreams have an expiration date*
> *if you don't act on them.*

If you stay on your current path, all of your dreams, aspirations, goals, pounds you want to lose, trips you want to take, and changes you want to make are never going to happen.

That is, if you don't dig in and become that bold and courageous person who wants to be unleashed on life. That's what it takes to make sure a brighter future is still ahead of you.

Don't let today be another day that you waste.

I write this, not from living a life in perfect Zen atop a mountain, drinking cloud-filtered water and sitting lotus-style, but from having wasted far too many days, months, and years. I write from experience spending a lot of time at brunches, drinking bottomless Mimosas, and talking about all the things I wanted to do instead of actually doing them. I write this from a place of once existing in fear and paralysis, seeking likes from social media posts or indifference from a glass of whiskey.

All of this may feel kind of harsh. Like, dude, chill on the tough love already. However, something tells me you don't need another patronizing pat on the back. Though it's hard to admit, you know these words speak some real truth. But as painful as these words may be to read, it kind of feels good, too, right?

That's because recognizing that time isn't infinite is actually an opportunity. It helps us to realize:

The moment of a lifetime is actually this moment that you're in right now.

No, you're not high on legal cannabis. That's just some good truth you smoked. This moment will never exist again.

Like most people, you probably have a really big dream inside of you. The challenge, and opportunity, is that you're nowhere near accomplishing that dream. Hell, maybe like I did, you even stopped dreaming at some point and just started going through the motions. Maybe you don't even know what you want from life anymore.

Or maybe you have a big goal you want to achieve. But month after month, year after year, you're nowhere close to crossing it off of your to-do list. What I'm talking about are those New Year's resolutions you make every year, but never seem to act on. (In fact, it's estimated that more than 80 percent of New Year's resolutions fail by February.)[2]

Our dreams, our goals, those things we say are important—they're like fruit you buy at the grocery store. They can get bruised, start to rot, and eventually, expire. Let me say this again:

Your dreams have an expiration date.

That's if—and this is a big if—you don't act on them.

There's an amazing Spanish proverb that goes, "Tomorrow is often the busiest day of the week." This is 100 percent true. How many times have you said, "I'll get to it tomorrow," without actually getting to it at all?

When you start to fret about not making progress on your

dreams and goals, that's when your friends, family, and coworkers will provide some of the absolute most god-awful (though well-meaning) advice to help you feel better about life, like:

"Maybe it just wasn't meant to be."

Was it not meant to be? Or did you give up?

Or, well-intentioned people will share four of the most deceptive words that can come out of someone's mouth:

"It's never too late."

Blasphemy! Here's the remix of "It's never too late" that a real friend, coach, or mentor would say to you:

"It's never too late, but the longer you wait, the harder it gets."

Why does it get harder? It's Newton's first law of motion. When referencing this law, most people focus on "an object in motion stays in motion . . ." But there's another part to this law: "an object at rest stays at rest."

So, if you're at home sitting on the couch, drinking spiked seltzers while binge-watching a television series that aired in the 1990s right now, there's a good chance you'll find yourself saying, "Maybe it just wasn't meant to be" in the future . . . unless you take action on your dreams now.

YOUR DREAMS NEED ENCOURAGEMENT

When Senator Barack Obama was considering running for president, he sought out the advice of other senior politicians.

Most told him he was too young and inexperienced to run for president.

But one senator[3] and advisor told him, "Never count on that window staying open." Obama's star was on the rise, and he knew that it might not last forever. There was a short time frame in which to make a decision—to run or not to run.

That crucial encouragement is how we came to know him as President Obama.

Right now, you have a window of opportunity, too. But if you don't move forward on your dreams and projects when the time is ripe, you could end up with nothing but regret.

At this very moment, there are people accomplishing great things. Are they smarter than you or do they know something you don't? Absolutely not. The only difference between you and them is that they're taking consistent steps forward every single day.

You can do this, too. But to make progress on your dreams and goals, know this:

Your dreams need encouragement.

Encouragement is the momentum that you create with your daily actions.

BELIEVE IN YOURSELF LIKE OTHERS DO

The first step to being bolder and better is learning to encourage yourself.

When I was in the sixth grade at Hunt Elementary, my teacher Mrs. Hirschman changed my life. At the time, things weren't going well for me at home. I was struggling to deal with my parents' divorce from a few years earlier and we seemed to be constantly moving to a new apartment in my small hometown. Everything felt unstable. My mother did her best, and it must have been tough raising three kids primarily by herself while working a full-time job.

During this time, I was sad and angry. To make matters worse, I was shy, insecure, and had low self-esteem. Then, Mrs. Hirschman showed up in my life. It was as if she knew I was headed toward turning into a proverbial bad apple if something didn't shift.

So, she did something that would change my life. Was it some selfless act of heroism? No. Mrs. Hirschman cast me in the lead role in the sixth-grade production of *The Nutcracker*.

I remember being so nervous as we rehearsed and prepared. I begged Mrs. Hirschman to cast someone else in the lead, but she wouldn't. Instead, she promised that she'd support me and that we'd work together to make sure I remembered all my lines.

As we prepared for the play, I wanted to quit countless times—but she wouldn't let me. And I'm grateful she didn't. On opening night, even with a few hiccups, the play went great. It was exhilarating and empowering being onstage. It was one of the first times I actually felt seen.

After our last performance, the cast came out to give an extra bow to the audience. Even with all of the parents and families clapping, the only person's reaction I looked for was Mrs. Hirschman's. It felt so good to know that she believed in me.

By casting me in that play, Mrs. Hirschman showed me what it meant to have someone believe in me. The by-product of this was that I learned to believe in myself when I needed it most. It helped me fully understand the life-changing power of belief.

Believe in yourself the way others do.

Unfortunately, I never got to tell Mrs. Hirschman what she did for me. When I looked her up a few years ago to say thank-you, I found out that she had died just a few months earlier. I can only imagine how many other kids like me she helped over the years.

Right now, think about that person who has truly believed in you during your life in a meaningful way. Someone who really made, or still is making, a positive impact on your life. Visualize them or write down their name.

Think about all the things they've done for you to help you succeed, move forward, and believe in yourself. I want you to write them a letter or an e-mail to thank them and let them know. Don't wait like I did until it's too late.

OLD STORIES

As we discussed earlier, the stories we tell ourselves about what we can and can't do can be very powerful. One of the hardest things about making a bold change is coming to terms with, and then saying goodbye to, our old stories that don't serve us. This is similar to the idea we explored in chapter 3, when we talked about the decisions in your life that you have yet to accept. I want to dig a little deeper here because these old stories, even more than a single decision we regret, can alter the course of our lives.

Old stories are the situations, circumstances, or experiences that happened to us in the past, outside of our control, that we still allow to hold power over our lives today. It's kind of like carrying around a heavy backpack that weighs you down and keeps you from moving.

The most common old story I've heard from my coaching clients over the years is about something difficult or painful that happened earlier in their life but that continues to prevent them from moving forward as an adult. These are the kind of old stories that leave a chip—or for some, a full-on fracture—on their shoulder that can stop them from making progress on what's important.

Maybe you've been the victim of abuse or harassment. Maybe you were treated poorly in a previous relationship and that affects the quality of your current relationship. Or, maybe you've experienced a traumatic accident that haunts you to this day. I've experienced this firsthand as well.

One of my old stories was that I was abandoned, physically and emotionally, as a child. The by-product of this story was that throughout my life, whenever good things would happen to me in my career or relationships, I'd typically engage in some type of self-sabotaging behavior without being fully aware of my actions. My old story would take over, and I would self-sabotage to "protect" myself from the chance that the rug would be pulled from underneath me once again.

It has taken many years and a lot of therapy and coaching sessions to release this old story. One of the most powerful experiences I ever had in my life was standing in front of a room full of strangers at a Hendricks Institute personal development workshop in Ventura, California. There I stood in the room, saying, "That was then, this is now," as I pointed behind me and then in front of me. I did this repeatedly until tears streamed down my face. I finally acknowledged that my old stories were in the past.

That was then, this is now.

Whatever your old story is, I invite you to embrace it, own it, and take the necessary steps required to release it. It's part of your story, but it's not your whole story. There's a lot of open road ahead of you.

Humbly, I acknowledge that this is easier said than done, and I invite you to seek professional support if your old story has become an albatross that has led to inaction, self-sabotage, or even addiction.

COMMIT AND RECOMMIT. EVERY. SINGLE. DAY.

Once we believe, we must commit. To ourselves. And to our dreams.

What's interesting is that in our society, we often talk about how important it is to commit to something. But here's something that conveniently goes left unsaid:

> *Once you commit to something,*
> *you have to recommit to it every day.*

When I played high school football, our head coach had the team repeat the same quote at the beginning and end of every practice. We'd say:

Good better best.

Never let it rest.

Until your good is your better, and your better is your best.

At the time, I thought it was just something catchy that rhymed. Now with experience, I see the true value in it and what he was trying to instill in us.

It's about being 100 percent committed and disciplined.

We live in an age when people like to wing it. In my experience, winging it is only easy if you're well prepared. Here's the thing: either you're committed, or you aren't. Yeah, I know, I can already hear someone saying, "Well, it's all relative."

But as motivational author and speaking legend Zig Ziglar once said, and I'm paraphrasing: if you're married, do you want your spouse to be *relatively* faithful?

So, what can get in the way of committing? FOMO—the fear of missing out and always thinking about hypothetical situations instead of what's right in front of you. Instead of FOMO, maybe think about the joy you'll feel when you move forward by committing.

WHY COMMITTING REALLY MATTERS

When I first began my speaking career, my agent asked if I was ready to deliver a keynote to more than three thousand people at a high-profile event in Pittsburgh. My inner doubts said, *Absolutely not. I'm a novice and I don't have nearly enough experience or hours under my belt to speak in front of that many people.* My inner doubts were absolutely correct. Still, I decided to go for it and said yes. Even though I prepared and told myself I could do it, the truth was that I was in over my head.

The event was a massive failure. I bombed. I stunk up the joint. Still, I remember getting a standing ovation, which confused the hell out of me. Later, I learned that the tradition was for the audience to give every speaker a standing ovation after their talk. Odds are, this tradition was canceled after my horrible performance.

That night, I exited the arena as fast as I could and found the closest bar. To this day, I still get embarrassed when I think about the experience. However, that moment of failure sparked something inside of me to ensure that I'd never bomb like that again. That night profoundly changed me as a speaker. It triggered my transition. I began taking the steps I needed to take to go from amateur to professional. It taught me that I couldn't just hope to be good, I had to do the work required to become better at my craft so I could expect to be good.

THE IVY LEAGUE WAY:
HOPE LESS, EXPECT MORE

An important component of being better and bolder is how we view our hopes versus our expectations.

When I was a kid, there were times when my mother would take me with her to discount department stores like Kmart or Value City to return clothing that didn't fit me or my siblings so she could get a refund. Rarely do I remember these trips ending well.

I remember feeling anxious on the drives to the store, knowing exactly how the situation could play out. We would walk over to the returns department and wait in line. When our number was called, at times my mother would walk up and kindly say to the sales associate, "Hi. I'm *hoping* to return these clothes I bought for my son. They don't fit him and I'd like a refund, please."

This led to an extended back-and-forth, with the sales associate questioning my mother and inspecting the clothes she wanted to return. I can still remember my feelings of stress and anxiety as they negotiated.

On good days, they'd accept the return and refund my mother's money. On other days, they would attempt to deny her, at which point she would tell the sales associate in no uncertain terms, "Don't make me act a fool up in here. You're going to refund me my money."

On these same trips to department stores, I also remember witnessing the exact opposite scenario play out. As we waited in line for our turn, the person ahead of us would walk up to the sales associate and simply say, or demand, "I'm returning these clothes. I'd like a refund."

Funny enough, typically no questions were asked, no garments were inspected. There was no back-and-forth between the sales associate and the customer. The associate would immediately give them their money back.

What I realized later was that there's a critical difference in these two approaches. Some approached the interaction *hoping* to get the refund. The others *expected* to get the refund.

This had a profound effect on me. For a good portion of my life, I hoped to receive things or hoped for things to happen as opposed to expecting them.

Throughout my life, I saw situations like this play out—particularly when I was a graduate student at Columbia University, an Ivy League institution in New York City.

Growing up in small-town Michigan, I didn't know what an Ivy League school was. Sure, I was familiar with Harvard. But somehow, society had already told me that places like that weren't for me.

For undergrad, as a first-generation college student, I attended Western Michigan University. Situated in Kalamazoo, this university turned out to be the perfect place for me to start to spread my wings and launch my life. But even back then, I felt inferior to friends who attended what I considered to be "brand name" schools like the University of Michigan.

When I was in my late twenties, I was considering shifting my career from the entertainment industry to journalism to make more of a difference and tell stories that mattered. A mentor suggested that I apply to Columbia University's Journalism School, an esteemed program. Immediately, I resisted this idea. Even though I'd come a long way from my humble upbringing and from Western Michigan University, a voice in my head said, *That's the Ivy League. That's for* them, *not you.*

Still, I applied. And lo and behold, I was accepted. I decided to hit "pause" on my career to head back to school.

When I arrived at that historic Morningside Heights campus in Manhattan, I immediately felt out of place. Even though I was in my late twenties at the time and had experienced some "success," I felt like a fraud in the classroom. I felt like that child standing next to my mother who was hoping to receive a refund. In other words, even though I had been accepted, I still felt like I didn't belong. To be clear, no one told me this. This is what I was telling myself.

After a few weeks, I found my footing and, slowly but surely, built my confidence. That's when I started to notice something I previously couldn't articulate. I call it the Ivy League Way.

From where I stood, pretty much everyone on that campus *expected* to be at Columbia University. Whether this was instilled in them from their upbringing or early education, I don't know. But it was clear that they felt that they were right where they should be, and they didn't seem to feel bad or guilty about it.

My experience was the exact opposite. I *hoped* to be there. Never mind that I had the credentials to be there. I felt as if I would be "found out" at any moment, and kicked out of school.

Then, something happened. As I began to excel in the classroom and started building relationships with students and professors, I realized there wasn't a difference between me and anyone else on campus. I could handle my own in the classroom and in intellectual debates. But I also seemed to have something that I perceived, rightly or wrongly, not a lot of my fellow classmates had—it's what you might call "street smarts," or grit. This experience helped me succeed and recalibrate my inner compass so it no longer pointed at hope, but rather pointed at expectation, and reset my approach to life

The difference between expecting and hoping is massive.

Expectation comes from a confident, active place: leaning forward, standing upright, being confident. Hope can come from an insecure, passive place: leaning back, hunching over, feeling unsure.

Don't get me wrong, there's a bad kind of expectation. When expectation morphs into entitlement and privilege, it can be ugly. But when expectation is fueled by doing the work required to get wherever you want to go, it's a powerful tool to have in your arsenal.

Being bold and committed requires you to expect more and hope less.

When you've committed and done the work, you can expect.

Saint Augustine once said, "Pray as though everything depended on God. Work as though everything depended on you." That, my friend, is positive expectation.

FIND THE CHILD INSIDE OF YOU

One last thought on being bolder and better. And it stems from becoming a dad.

Having children will profoundly change your life. *Really, Captain Obvious?* you're probably thinking. But my kids continue to change my life in a variety of surprising ways.

A therapist once told me, "Your children will be your teachers." It took some time to fully understand and appreciate the point he was making.

My toddler son is an amazing teacher. From what my wife and I can gather so far, this dude has no fear. He approaches life with joy, adventure, and a pure impulse to explore that simultaneously delights me and freaks me out.

While most kids lose it on the first day of preschool and hold on tight to a parent's leg, my son didn't think twice about walking into that classroom. On the street, he stops strangers to say hello and ask the name of their dog. If he sees a snake while we're out on a hike, he chases after it before it can chase after him. Climbing into and jumping from trees (or cabinets, or bookshelves), no matter the risk, gives him unabashed delight. His curiosity in a new space is captivating and he easily gets lost in new sights and sounds. He has an energy, zest, and love for life that blows me away.

While our son is the adventurer of the family, his twin sister is the comedian and performer. She's always trying to make us laugh with silly faces or by coming up with ridiculous new sounds. In her world, performing, being funny, and having a good time reign supreme. When around family and friends, she regularly invites others to play and wants everyone to be involved. Blessed with a great imagination, she creates fantastic stories and has a personality that makes you want to be playful and silly.

Our daughter is also the helper of the family. When her mother or I am preparing a meal, she always pulls up a stool to the counter and finds a way to contribute. And when it comes to playing, she finds joy in creating things. The commitment and imagination she brings to the table when she's building a castle with her stackable blocks always amazes me. Even when they fall and she has to start over, she's so focused that she rarely seems fazed and immediately starts reconstructing her next masterpiece.

When I compare my kids' upbringing with my own, it's hard not to let years of social conditioning get the best of me.

Unlike my kids, I approached my early life with fear, trepidation, and a "What can go wrong?" kind of outlook. Instead of seeing the joy in everything, for far too long, I only saw the potential hurt or disappointment.

Unfortunately, at times I've caught myself trying to rein in my kids' natural zest for life with discipline, conformity, and control—the things that I thought would keep them safe. It was like I was trying to tame wild stallions and take away what makes them special. I struggled with being a conscious parent.

The balance between allowing a child to be who they are while teaching them how to be in the world is delicate. We don't want to take away their joy of living and spontaneity. Simultaneously, we don't want their young, impressionable minds (housed in squishy, vulnerable bodies) to think it's cool to put a knife in an electrical socket to see what happens.

So, where's the balance? I once heard someone say, "If you're not having fun, it doesn't count." I have to remind myself of this regularly. It guides how I approach parenting. And it's the most important lesson my kids teach me every single day.

Now, remember when you were a kid. The joy you had. The wonder you lived with. The excitement of seeing something for the first time. Somewhere deep inside of us, even though that kid is now an adult, this sense of play still exists. Unfortunately, most of us have buried it under years of social conditioning.

Today, I invite all of us to reframe the situations we are in and ask ourselves if we can approach them with childlike wonder. To see things the way you would with a child's eyes. To ask *why* more. To take more risks. To have more fun. To live more boldly. Only then, can we live better.

NEXT STEPS

1. What is it about the "old days" or the "old you"
    that you miss?

2. If your life were a movie, and the movie was
    halfway over, what would the lead character start
    doing to turn things around?

3. Who has believed in you during your life? What
    did they do to show you their belief?

4. What window could close if you don't take action?
    What steps do you need to take to keep the
    possibility of this dream alive?

6

WHAT DO YOU WANT?

"Your mission is your priority. Unless you know your mission and have aligned your life to it, your core will feel empty."

—DAVID DEIDA, *THE WAY OF THE SUPERIOR MAN*

WHAT DO YOU want? We hear this seemingly simple question constantly throughout our lives—so often that it can mask the deceptive complexity of it. It requires being in tune with ourselves, our likes and dislikes, and knowing how to vocalize them.

And one day, that simple question caught me off guard.

It was about 7:30 a.m. on a Tuesday quite a few years back at the 18th Street Coffee House in Santa Monica. Somehow, even though I was in line to order at a coffee shop, I wasn't prepared to answer the barista's question. It felt heavy.

"What do you want?" she asked from behind the counter.

The bluntness and tone of her question caused me to freeze. Was she asking me about my beverage choice or something bigger?

She smiled and I smiled back uncomfortably.

Before I could respond, she said again, "Sooo, *what* do you want?"

"Uh, large coffee," I said to the barista-slash-life-coach.

A few moments later, she handed me my coffee and smiled. "Good luck," she said, which was an extremely odd thing for a barista to say.

What does she know that I don't? I thought, as I walked to a booth.

At that time in my life, I didn't know exactly what I wanted. When I wasn't working, I went wherever the day my e-mail inbox took me. For all intents and purposes, I was on cruise control, coasting through my life as if I didn't have—or want to have—a say in anything happening in my life.

Her question, the simplicity of it, triggered something deep inside of me. It's one of the most challenging simple questions you can be asked: "What do you want?"

Now, I'm going to ask you the same question:

What do you want?

YOU CAN DO ANYTHING YOU WANT, BUT . . .

Before you attempt to answer the question posed above, let me tell you about when graduate school was winding down for me in New York City in 2006. I was faced with the same issue as just about every other new grad: what to do next with my life.

At the time, I wanted to take the summer off and travel the world. I wanted to write a book. I wanted to create and sell a television show. I wanted to create and host a podcast. I wanted a job as a reporter with a top cable news network. I wanted to start my own business. I wanted to produce a documentary. I wanted to do *every* damn thing.

One day over coffee at a Turkish café on Amsterdam Avenue in the Morningside Heights neighborhood of Manhattan, I shared this with a professor who had become a mentor. He kindly listened as I told him all of the things that I wanted to do.

When I finished, he looked at me, smiled, and said something I will never forget:

"You can do anything you want, but you can't do everything."

This was exactly what I didn't want to hear. His answer pissed me off. Why? Because he was right. And now, I'm going to tell you the exact same thing that he told me:

You can do anything you want, but you can't do everything.

For far too long, since we were old enough to comprehend words, we've been told and encouraged with these words: "You can do anything!"

Don't get me wrong. I appreciate the optimism. But the next time you give a nine-year-old, or heck, a forty-three-year-old, this impassioned advice—"You can do anything you want!"—you must then look them directly in the eyes and say:

"To be clear, you can do anything, but you can't do *everything*. You're going to have to choose. That is what's going to separate you from everyone else, if you're up for it."

Then, take a long sip of whatever you're drinking, pat them on the top of their head, and walk away like a boss.

In this multihyphenate day and age, far too many people are trying to do everything.

When you try to do everything, most times you end up accomplishing nothing.

Whenever I find myself getting distracted with unimportant things that are actually steering me away from what I care about most, that conversation with my professor plays in my mind.

DON'T SET YOURSELF UP FOR A CRASH

Speaking of having too much going on, back in my college days, the popular drink at bars and clubs was the infamous Long Island Iced Tea. This "cocktail"—if you want to offend great bartenders everywhere and call it that—has seemingly *every* type of alcohol in it. Vodka, gin, tequila, rum, and triple sec, mixed with splashes of cola and sour mix.

Far too many times in my youth, more times than I care to admit, this was my drink of choice as well. Beware: when someone orders this at the bar, they are on a mission, and one mission alone—to get hammered.

The by-product of imbibing this horrid drink, the drink that is trying to be *everything,* is knowing that you'll almost certainly crash, burn—and yes, vomit—later in the evening. Odds are this vomiting will take place in the back seat of someone else's car.

Don't be that person who orders a Long Island Iced Tea.

In many ways, life can be like a Long Island Iced Tea. We're throwing too many things into the mix. Too many apps are open in our operating system of life. Work. Projects. Obligations.

You know what happens when you have too many apps open on a computer or smartphone? Your operating speed slows down. Apps that you are actively using start to freeze because the other unused or minimized apps are sucking up all the energy, running behind the scenes without our knowledge—without even being useful. After a while, worst-case scenario, you may experience a major crash and lose everything you've been working on.

Life is no different. And, let me tell you, I know about crashes all too well.

Toward the end of my television career in New York City around 2011, I was a correspondent for a high-profile business web series produced by NBC. I was also a correspondent for a news program targeting high school students and I regularly hosted a pop culture web show with the unfortunate name *Hot-Newz*. On top of that, I was self-producing and hosting a TV pilot that I hoped to sell to a network. I should also add that I was enjoying being single, that along with all that New York City had to offer.

During this time, a major talent agency in Hollywood that had big plans for me wanted to sign me. But in the midst of overstretching myself, I allowed this rare opportunity to pass me by. Months later, when I looked up and everything that I was juggling had failed to materialize, I had nowhere to turn—no more options to pursue. Just like seven years earlier when I got fired from my job at Nickelodeon, I crashed hard. The wreckage was of my own making (the way most wreckages are). When I called that big-time Hollywood agency to see if they were still interested in working with me, they wouldn't even take my call.

But sometimes a crash serves as a reminder that it's time to delete the apps in our lives that no longer serve us. In my case, I needed to assess which commitments were overwhelming my life, wasting my time, and taking up all my valuable bandwidth.

HOW MANY APPS DO YOU HAVE OPEN?

How many apps do you currently have open in your life? Are you attempting to do *everything*?

"Apps" could be jobs, hobbies, special projects, kids, housework, friends, caregiving, volunteer obligations, social appointments, and so forth. When we have too many apps open, there's a lot of "I'm sooo busy" going on, but nothing actually gets done.

When we have too many apps open, we become so distracted we don't have a true litmus test of how we feel. Countless research studies have confirmed that our brains were not designed for multitasking. Many of us have yet to fully embrace how important it is to guard our time and be selective about what we say yes to.

Take a moment and grab a blank piece of paper or open up a Google doc. Write down all of the "apps," or in-progress projects and responsibilities, in your life. Identify which of those projects are just depleting your energy. Jot them all down and watch your blank piece of paper or screen quickly fill up.

Now, one by one, review all of your open apps and ask yourself if they really matter.

Which apps need to stay open? Which apps need to be closed for the foreseeable future? And which need to go in the trash once and for all? If you had to choose just one app to stay open, which would it be?

If the idea of choosing just one scares you, ask yourself *why* it scares you. If you're honest with yourself, you'll learn a lot from the answer.

In functional medicine, sometimes doctors recommend that patients do an elimination diet if they're experiencing health issues. This is where you remove certain foods, like sugar, gluten, or dairy, from your diet. Then, after a certain amount of time, you slowly reintroduce the foods one by one. Only then can you really know which foods are making you ill. But the first step is elimination.

If you're not sure where to start, try eliminating a low-priority task that's been a consistent thorn in your side and see how you feel. For example, maybe you feel an obligation to post weekly to a blog that you stopped caring about long ago. Or maybe each week, you get together with a group of friends to throw a few drinks back, but you do it solely out of obligation. Or maybe you've become the go-to person to give people rides to or from the airport, even with the existence of ride-sharing services. It could even be that nonprofit whose mission you really care about, but that takes up more and more of your time than you were truly hoping to give.

Once you experiment with eliminating some "apps," even small ones, gauge your mood, your health, and even your excitement, or trepidation, to start each day. In my experience, you'll find that once you identify which apps need to be closed in your life, you'll have more energy, focus, and clarity. A powerful question to ask yourself is:

"What are you willing to give up to live the life that you say you want?"

The truth that most of us are afraid to acknowledge is that some things really do matter more than others. Knowing the difference between what does and doesn't matter will profoundly change your life for the better.

Now, let's dig deeper into some of the recurring themes in your life that might be holding you back from determining what you're ready to give up.

WHAT YOUR LIFE AND A HOLLYWOOD CASTING DEPARTMENT HAVE IN COMMON

You know those people who always seem to have challenges with their boss or coworkers, no matter where they work? This story follows them everywhere.

Do you know people whose friends or family members have regularly let them down to the point where it doesn't surprise you? This behavior has become standard, not abnormal.

Or, maybe you know someone who, like clockwork, has something get in the way (again) of finishing that passion project?

And maybe, just maybe, you know someone whose newest relationship ended just like the last one because they didn't fully trust their partner?

Is it possible that the person I reference in these examples is you? Are there other roles that you recognize yourself playing, over and over again in your life?

In my experience, life is like a Hollywood casting department. It has a funny, not-so-funny way of casting certain things, people, and experiences into your life. These things, people, and experiences (particularly the challenging or bad ones) keep showing up over and over again until we learn what we most need to learn from them and are finally willing to make different choices.

Think about the past few years of your life—or heck, just the last thirty days. What did these years or days have in common? Do you notice any recurring themes? Are there people or experiences that have regularly showed up? Sure, these could be themes that appear in your life to help you. But more times than not, they get in the way and keep you where you are.

Let's take another cue from Hollywood with this question:

If your life during the last year had been a movie,
what genre would it be?

Comedy

Action

Drama

Adventure

Romance

Sadly, for far too many people, life is a drama—sometimes because of forces outside of their control, but often because of their own hang-ups.

As an entrepreneur client of mine recounted, for as long as she could remember, her life at the office was a drama. Repeatedly, she experienced conflict with the employees she hired and eventually had to fire them.

It wasn't until she truly evaluated her tendencies that she realized she regularly hired employees at low wages who didn't have the skill sets the job actually required. She ultimately accepted that she needed to offer higher salaries to attract and retain talented people who were great fits for their jobs. Now she experiences far less friction and drama, and her company earns more revenue.

Life may not be a movie, but you do get to write the script. So, let's name you—not just as the screenwriter, but also as the new head of your casting department. We're going to put the control back in your hands. The first step is getting clear on what you want. Otherwise, life is going to cast whatever or whomever comes along.

Starting in this chapter, we're going to make intentional decisions to "cast" the right things, people, and experiences into your life. The question begs:

If this next year of your life were a movie, what genre would you like it to be?

Before we explore your answer, let's look at one other recurring theme in our lives—our complaints.

OUR COMPLAINTS OPEN A WINDOW

What do you regularly complain about?

Think about your day-to-day. When you're out with friends or at home with your boo, do you have conversations or *complaint sessions*? There's a big difference.

If your answer is that you don't complain, you're not telling the truth. My guess is that you probably complain far more than you think. If you don't know what you complain about, just ask your family or friends. They will gladly answer. Just make sure you give yourself enough time. It might take a while.

My friend, author Jon Gordon, wrote a great book called *The No Complaining Rule*. It's about the positive ways to deal with negativity.

The book is simultaneously a great and challenging read because it makes the reader evaluate what role they've played in their own unhappiness and how much complaining seeps into their everyday lives.

The thing about complaining is that no matter how good it feels while you're doing it, it zaps your energy and sinks you deeper into whatever hole you're already in. Still, I believe we can find value with our complaints. They can provide deep insight into what we really want.

I once heard the quote:

"Sometimes the things we complain most about are the things we care most about."

So, what do you regularly complain about? For example, here are five areas of my life that I regularly complain about:

1. Money

2. Time

3. Marriage

4. Health

5. Career

Now, list the top five categories you regularly complain about. Pick a category where you play an active role—as opposed to, say, complaining about spicy food or rush-hour traffic.

1.

2.

3.

4.

5.

Now, as you look at your complaints, ask yourself an adult question: "What does complaining about these things do for me?"

Here are my answers:

1. *Money:* When I complain about not saving enough money or not being as financially disciplined as I'd like to be, it provides me with permission to feel sorry for myself instead of regularly meeting with our gifted financial advisor.

2. *Time:* When I complain about not having enough time to do everything that I'd like to accomplish over the course of my day, it provides me with an easy out so I don't have to take accountability for wasting time on social

media or for not getting up thirty minutes earlier each morning.

3. *Marriage:* When I complain about the challenges of marriage or something my wife does, I'm expecting her to change or do something differently. This provides me with a feeling of being right, as opposed to having to change myself, have compassion, or shift perspectives.

4. *Health:* When I complain about being out of shape and not having as much energy as I'd like, it provides me with a chance to be lazy—to focus on the problem instead of the solution, like making better food choices when I'm on the road for work.

5. *Career:* When I complain about having to send invoices, process expense reports, or follow up on money owed to me, it provides me with excuses for why I can't book more speaking engagements—because I'm just too busy doing administrative duties.

Now you. What do your complaints provide for you?

1.

2.

3.

4.

5.

Typically, complaining provides us with three things:

It stops us from taking personal accountability.

It places the blame on someone else or an outside situation.

It leaves things as they are, focusing on the problem rather than creative solutions.

Remember: children complain but adults take responsibility for the roles they play. Sadly, complaining has become the norm, not the exception, in our society. In fact, complaining is seemingly why social media was invented.

HOW TO STOP COMPLAINING

I have some great news for you. There's a simple way to stop complaining in its tracks and instead make progress on what matters.

The next time you find yourself in a conversation with a friend or family member who never stops complaining, simply ask them this direct question:

"I hear you that you don't like [whatever they're complaining about]. So, what do you want?"

If the question doesn't work the first time and they just keep on complaining, be persistent. Ask again:

"What do you want?"

This question is like a Taser to the chest. It shocks you and stops you in your tracks.

Typically, the response to this question will be a stalling technique: "What do you mean, what do I want?" Follow up with:

"What do you want that will stop you from complaining?" (If you want to piss them off, just for fun, smile after you ask this.)

Odds are, they'll get mad, change the subject, or go find someone else to complain to.

What many people seem to want today is an argument, not an outcome.

Don't be that person. Get curious. Find a solution. Make a

plan. Go after what you *do* want as opposed to focusing on what you don't.

To be sure, it's worth noting that when some people who are close to us "complain," they're solely looking to be heard and process things out loud. They may not even want a solution and thirty minutes later, they'll be just fine. It's our job to use our emotional intelligence to determine what the person we're communicating with most needs at that moment, and to be truthful about our own needs.

WHAT'S YOUR PLAN?

Now, back to an earlier question I asked you:

If this next year of your life were a movie,
what genre would you like it to be?

Comedy
Action
Drama
Adventure
Romance

When I asked myself this question back in 2016, at one of my lowest points, what I craved was a life of action, of forward momentum. I wanted to tackle things head-on instead of just waiting for something to happen.

As you think about and articulate your answer, I invite you to choose just one genre. Two movie genres mixed together can get a bit weird—like *Abraham Lincoln: Vampire Hunter* or *Pride and Prejudice and Zombies*.

Now that you've selected your genre, let's consider some rapid-fire questions to ponder:

What do you want from today?

What do you want from this week?

What do you want for your health?

What do you want for your relationships?

What do you want for your finances?

What do you want for your career?

What. Do. You. Want?

Unfortunately, we spend a lot of time staying busy and in motion. But we rarely end up where we want to be. This is because we never stop to ask ourselves these straightforward questions.

This is the equivalent of just getting into a car and driving without a destination in mind and with no GPS. You could end up anywhere. And most people do. They end up exactly where they didn't want to be because they never took the time to ask where they *did* want to go.

To make progress toward what matters, you first have to know what matters.

I get it. It's scary to pick a single direction. But while keeping our options open might seem like an easier path to follow, it's not really a path at all. It's simply not making a decision.

What is keeping all of your options open actually costing you?

Or, to put it another way, what is that good situation of yours—also known as the "golden handcuffs"—really costing you? Maybe it's staying in a rent-controlled apartment in a neighborhood where you don't want to live, just because it's cheap. That good situation could be costing you the life you truly envisioned for yourself.

Staking a claim, making a decision, and choosing something to pursue isn't easy. If it was, more people would do it. But if you don't want to lead a life of inaction, you must act. What are you missing by *not* committing to a course of action?

SO, WHAT *DO* YOU WANT?

I would normally say that the next step is for you to list all of the things that you *don't* want in your life—just to get the juices flowing.

People often say, "It's just as important to know what you don't want as it is to know what you do want." Indeed, there is some value to that statement, but for today we're going to ignore it. I'm not going to let you off that easy.

I want you to answer the question: *What do you want?* Do you want to spend your life wondering, or do you really want something?

For this first round, there are no wrong answers. I want you to get used to making decisions and staking claims. Never forget:

Not making a decision is making a decision.

Think deep and hard about what you *do* want in your life. Open up a journal or a Google doc. Write twenty-five statements that begin with, "I want . . ." and finish them. I don't care what you write. The key is to focus on what you *do* want. Even if it's outlandish, silly, or offensive, write it down.

You can start with, "I want my back hair removed . . ." "I want to throw away all of my coworkers' old food in the office refrigerator . . ." "I want to travel to Tokyo . . ." "I want to earn more money . . ."

For now, don't worry about getting too specific. It's okay if you write, "I want to make more money" versus "I want to make $34,765.98 more this year than I did last year."

There's one caveat. The "I want . . ." statements must be things over which you have primary control. They can't exist in that gray area where success or failure is dependent upon someone else.

So, "I want Debra to be nicer to me" isn't allowed. You have zero control over what Debra does or doesn't do. I mean, come on, it's *Debra* we're talking about.

I'll start with ten examples:

1. *I want to make more money.*

2. *I want my kids to eat their vegetables.*

3. *I want to spend a year abroad.*

4. *I want to work with a personal trainer.*

5. *I want to wake up every day at 5:00 a.m.*

6. *I want to pay off my mother's mortgage.*

7. *I want to have more sex with my wife.*

8. *I want to have an annual guys trip.*

9. *I want to pay off my graduate school debt.*

10. *I want to be in the best physical shape ever.*

Now, it's your turn to write those twenty-five "I want . . ." statements.

It's important to come up with twenty-five "I want . . ." statements as opposed to five or ten, because it allows your brain to flex its muscle and not be limited. Further, if you limit yourself to just five, you could be truly missing out on something powerful that could be uncovered with more digging. Once again, don't stop till you've given it your best shot. Seriously, do it. I'll wait.

BUT WHY?

Congratulations on coming up with your twenty-five "I want . . ." statements.

Now, out of those twenty-five, select the five that really speak to you. They're the real deal. They're within your control. If they happened, you would truly be stoked.

Don't worry if there are more than five that make you feel alive. They'll always be there later. For now, start with five.

For the next step, I want you to find your inner kid. That annoying kid who always asks why. For your top five "I want . . ." statements, your next step is to identify the why behind each of them. Why do you want what you want?

The best way to identify your true why behind a statement is by asking yourself why five times. Sakichi Toyoda, the founder of Toyota Industries, developed this process in the 1930s and many companies use it today to solve problems.

I'll start with my example of: *I want to make more money.*

Next, you ask yourself *why* five times.

1. "Why do you want to make more money?"

I want to make more money, so money isn't a concern in my life.

2. "Why do you want money not to be a concern in your life?"

Because it creates stress and anxiety.

3. "Why does it create stress and anxiety?"

Because I have a family that I'm responsible for and I don't want to let them down.

4. *"Why don't you want to let them down?"*

Because taking care of and providing for my family is the most important thing to me.

5. *"Why is taking care of and providing for your family the most important thing to you?"*

Because growing up, I experienced a lot of instability and I want my kids to never have to worry about that and to always feel safe.

As you probably noticed from my example, the first why isn't enough. Nor is the second, third, or fourth. What you get with the fifth why is the goodness. The real answer. That's because it requires us to dig deep and go below the surface.

The first answer most people give to deep questions is what I call the leaf on the tree. Our job is to go from the leaf to the twig to the branch to the trunk to the roots. That's where we find our real why.

What's fascinating about the answer to my fifth why question is that ensuring that my kids "never have to worry and always feel safe" isn't solely reliant on my earning more money. What I really want isn't necessarily more money, but to be able to be there for my kids. To be a stable presence in their life. This is something my parents couldn't provide for me. This is very different from my statement of wanting to make more money. I can do this even if I never earn more than I do today.

Once we acknowledge why we really want something, how we view it can totally change. Sure, I can make more money. But being there for my kids is priceless.

This "five whys" exercise can be a game changer in your life and career. It can help you understand not only what you want, but also why you crave a certain outcome.

What I've yet to share with you, dear reader, is why we're doing these exercises. We're doing this because:

> **No one can help you, and you can't help yourself, if you don't know what you want.**

Even if what you've identified so far isn't "it," you're well on your way.

NEXT STEPS

1. If your life during the last year were a movie, what genre would it have been? If your life during the next year were a movie, what genre would you like it to be and why?

2. What do you regularly complain about? What do your complaints provide you with?

3. What do you want? List twenty-five things over which you have control.

4. Pick your top five from the statements created above. Do the "five whys" exercise with each statement.

PART TWO

BE THE PERSON YOU'RE SUPPOSED TO BE

7

STOP LIVING ON AUTOPILOT

*"You wanna fly, you got to give up
the shit that weighs you down."*

—TONI MORRISON, *SONG OF SOLOMON*

WHEN I WAS a kid, I remember looking in awe at men who I thought were successful.

One thing these "successful" men all had in common was the clothes they wore to work: brown dress slacks or khakis; a crisply starched, white button-down dress shirt; loafers with tassels on them; and, of course, for the pièce de résistance, a blue blazer with gold buttons. And if they were really successful, the buttons on the blazer had an anchor on them.

For a kid with a blue-collar upbringing and limited life experience outside of my Midwest hometown, this wardrobe meant success. It meant wealth. It meant having a family that was together. It meant taking vacations. It meant living on a different side of town—the good side. It meant having a home with an attached garage. It meant that you had it all figured out. This wardrobe symbolized a world that was far away from my upbringing and daily reality.

Growing up, my father worked in factories, so I always had a glimpse of what blue-collar, get-your-hands-dirty work looked like. But the other kind of work that some men did—where their hands didn't get dirty, where they didn't have to clock in at the beginning and end of their shift, and where it wasn't mandatory to wear a Dickies work shirt with their name on it—that work was foreign to me.

Now and then, I'd catch a glimpse of the white-collar professionals at my mother's office, where she worked as an administrative assistant. From as early as I could remember, I always felt out of place around these men. My eyes would be fixed on the floor in their presence, looking up just to peer into their world. But the one thing I knew was that one day, I wanted to wear the clothes that these "successful" men put on in the mornings.

I daydreamed that when I wore that wardrobe one day it would mean that somehow—against all the odds—I, Tony Neves, had made it.

That *I* was successful.

That *I* had figured it all out.

That *I* mattered.

If this bland uniform was the path to success, come hell or high water I was going to get it. However, one thing I neglected to ask myself back then was if these men were actually happy.

Fast-forward to the mid-1990s, I had landed an internship in Detroit, Michigan. This was a big deal for me. At the time, I thought Detroit was the be-all and end-all. In my world, technically it was. This was when the population of the Motor City was nearly one million people (today it's less than seven hundred thousand), the auto industry was still doing well, and the middle class was thriving.

I can still remember getting ready for the first day of my internship. I looked at myself in the mirror with pride. There I was wearing khaki pants, a button-up white shirt, maroon loafers (with tassels, of course), and finally, my stepfather's oversized blue blazer with gold buttons (but no anchors).

As I looked myself up and down in the full-length mirror, I attempted to conjure up a smile. I remember trying to get myself excited and thinking, *Tony, you've made it!* But something didn't feel right.

Instead of feeling like I'd made it, I felt like an actor getting dressed for a role in a straight-to-DVD movie. Still, I pushed my doubts aside and wore my uniform that whole summer. Ironically, not a single day passed that summer when I actually felt comfortable in those clothes. This was my first taste of conforming and starting to lose my personal identity to follow the crowd.

WHAT IS A UNIFORM?

A uniform doesn't necessarily have to be a physical wardrobe. It can be anything that you do routinely without question—or more than likely, without awareness—that gets in the way of being your true self.

A uniform can be a fixed mindset, or it can mean staying on the road when exiting would serve you best. It can mean doing something the same way because "that's how it's always been done."

A uniform can mean judging others for not wearing a uniform, or even nodding your head in agreement when you disagree with what's being said. It can be going deep into debt to buy a home that you can't afford, even though the bank approved the loan. It can be driving a fancy vehicle to keep up appearances.

A uniform can be holding on to someone or something (a belief, a city, a job, and so forth) that no longer serves your best interests because it's all you know. Alternatively, it can be the excuses and stories that you tell yourself about why things are the way they are in your life.

As members of society, we impose uniforms on ourselves when we stop being bold and courageous and begin following someone else's plan for our own lives.

To be clear, uniforms are suggested and encouraged by society. Since the birth of organized religion and periods like the industrial revolution, society has benefited from conformity. In fact, at one time, you were rewarded for wearing a uniform. You were accepted as a member of your community. You could get an education. You could get a good job. You could get a loan and buy a home. You could raise a family. You could retire and receive a gold watch or pen. You could receive a pension. And you could die in peace, knowing you did what you were supposed to do.

But times have changed.

In the twenty-first century, the by-products of wearing the uniform can include drowning in student debt or being laid off from your job with no severance while exiting CEOs receive multimillion-dollar packages. It can be foreclosure on your home during an economic recession when you found yourself unable to make your monthly payments to the bank (the same bank that was bailed out by the government). It can mean never being able to retire and working a full-time job into your seventies, not because you want to but because you have to. It can be not getting the pension or social security you paid into for all of those years. At worst, it can be losing everything due to medical bills simply because you, or someone you love, got sick. The list goes on and on.

Here's what I know, and what more and more people are figuring out, sometimes the hard way: *conforming and following the rules that society has created for us is exhausting.* Many of the uniforms imposed by society are ruining countless lives. No longer are there any guarantees.

WHAT UNIFORM DO YOU WEAR?

Now it's time to think about the uniform that you may wear every day to conform to an idea of "how things are supposed to be."

Be patient if you can't think of immediate answers. Some of us have been hiding behind a uniform for so long that we don't even know we're wearing it.

Here are a few powerful questions to let percolate in your brain:

Is your uniform a wardrobe like the one I once wore? Maybe your uniform is a point of view that isn't authentic to your core beliefs. Or, it could be the church that you attend weekly that has pivoted in a direction and espouses views that you no longer agree with.

Where did you learn to wear this uniform? Was it from society, family, friends, the education system, or your religion?

What does your uniform provide you? Is it money, safety, status, or security?

Knowing what you now know about life, does your uniform still serve you and your goals?

Who are you without the uniform?

And lastly, one of the most important questions you'll read in this book:

What is following the same path as everyone else costing you?

THE HARDEST ADVICE TO FOLLOW

The "guardrails" that a uniform provides can make us feel safe and secure. Of course, breaking away from the path of the uniform to pursue self-actualization, and being our truest self, isn't always easy. Hell, just look at how small the self-actualization pyramid is on top of Abraham Maslow's hierarchy of needs. As I know firsthand, some of the toughest advice to act on is to "just be yourself" and shed the uniform, especially when you don't have any support systems or a solid foundation to fall back on. To complicate matters further, you're not sure what "being yourself" will cost you.

During my time working in the television industry as a correspondent, reporter, and host, I developed the "reporter voice" that you've probably heard pretty much 100 percent of reporters use—whether they're on television or the radio.

The "reporter voice" is that affected, fake voice that sounds more like an automaton than a real-life human. Over the years, I can't tell you how many times family and friends would say to me, "Why do you talk like that when you're on camera?"

I never really had a response. *I thought that's how reporters were supposed to talk.*

Here's the truth. Talk to pretty much any reporter when they're *not* on the air and they sound nothing like they do on TV. In fact, they're rarely themselves on the air. They're playing the role of reporter and doing their best to speak with authority even if they sound like every other reporter. Been there, done that.

So why did I do it for all those years? And why do so many reporters and public speakers continue to talk in that contrived voice? Sure, it's easy to blame it on the job. But I've found that the real reason is more surprising:

It can be vulnerable to be the real you.

This is why the uniform shows up.

Over the years, something I would regularly hear from producers or directors during my television career was "Just be yourself." Maybe you've heard this advice over the course of your life as well.

Whenever I heard that—and I heard it a lot—I'd wonder, *Myself?! Who the hell is that? It's far easier to just talk in this fake voice instead.*

> *Speaking in an inauthentic voice is easy.*
> *Talking in your real voice, taking a stand*
> *for something, takes courage.*

Objectively speaking, I had a successful career in the highly competitive television industry that lasted more than ten years. I came a long way from arriving in New York City with about $800 in my bank account and with no connections to speak of, to working with some major national networks. Still, during my career, I had lots of meetings with television network executives and was considered for those big jobs where everyone gets to know your name. But I never did land one of those coveted high-profile jobs—and I truly believe it's because of the uniform I wore and how uncomfortable I was in my skin. I never showed them what I was really made of.

YOU ARE ALREADY VERIFIED

We can observe dynamics similar to the role of the uniform playing out in the social media world when you see a blue check mark symbol next to someone's username. This means that they are "verified."

Being verified means that, in some shape or form, the person is a public figure, celebrity, or global brand. For some, the verified badge is simply a uniform they wear.

Once after a public-speaking engagement at a university, a student came up to me and asked, "How do I get verified on Twitter like you?"

The question caught me off guard because no one had ever asked me this before. Though I intellectually knew the answer of how to get the blue check mark you see on Twitter, Facebook, Instagram, and other platforms, the question made me curious about the student.

"Tell me more about your question," I said to the student. "Why do you want to be 'verified?'"

The student hesitated and then responded, "I want to get verified to show that it's me."

This got me curious. "Is there another you that I should be aware of?" I asked. The student smiled.

"Well, no," the student said.

"Well, what is it then? Why do you want to be verified?" I asked.

"I just want to show that I'm important," the student responded.

The word *important* stopped me in my tracks. I immediately felt like I knew this student and the validation he craved.

I remembered leaving my job selling cheese in Florida and moving to New York City with dreams of breaking into the television industry. My goal was to "be on TV." For me, that was the equivalent of being verified. Of being accepted, even wanted. Like that student, I was craving something external that I didn't know could only be found within.

I looked the student directly in the eyes and said, "I want

you to know something. No blue check mark can 'verify' you. You verify you. You were verified the day that you were born."

The student nodded and thanked me for my time. I'm sure that wasn't the answer he wanted to hear, but I believe it was the answer he needed to hear. It was a message I wish someone had told me years ago. His blue badge was my blue blazer.

HOW TO START REMOVING THE UNIFORM

One of the major challenges that we face these days is how simple it is to live life on *autopilot.*

Robot vacuum cleaners can clean your living room floor for you. Streaming services like Netflix or Hulu can select shows for you, even before you pick up the remote. Groceries can be delivered to your front door by simply placing an order on an app. Playlists are made for you on Spotify so you can fool people into thinking you have good taste in music. Why walk to your next location when you can drive or hop on an electric scooter? Hell, the twenty-first-century car—with its AI autonomous driving, slick computer screens, sophisticated software, Wi-Fi, GPS navigation, Bluetooth, automatic starters, and steering-wheel and seat warmers—is basically a moving spa.

Everything's automatic. But here's the thing:

You were not made
to live on autopilot.
You are destined to be
the captain of your life.

You have the opportunity to shed your uniform and stop living on autopilot by *shifting gears*. It's time to define what life looks like on your terms. And, you have more gears available to you than you think. It's just that you might not know how to use them.

At one time, driving a car used to take a lot of effort and expertise. Pretty much up until the 1950s, the only type of car you could drive was a stick shift. There was no automatic. Even today, most cars have five to six gears—but in automatic and computerized cars, the engine is shifting without you even knowing it. However, if you've ever driven a stick shift, you know what it means to truly shift gears.

So how do you get unstuck? How do you get out of the automatic uniform mode in life and learn how to shift gears? The first step is picking one pattern and breaking it, no matter how simple it might seem.

Want to stop silly arguments with your spouse or partner? Maybe instead of "telling it like it is" or getting defensive when they point out something that you've done wrong, start asking questions that create a connection instead of disconnection. Get curious. Listen to learn more.

Want to stop being late everywhere you go? Next time, don't make hollow promises to yourself. Instead, set a timer to get out fifteen minutes earlier than you normally would.

Want to save more money? Start by picking one night this week to cook a meal at home instead of ordering takeout.

Want to start finally tackling that dream project you always said you'd finish? Get on YouTube and watch videos to learn how to do that thing you don't know how to do. Today. Make yourself accountable.

Want to finally finish that college degree that's been hanging over your head for years? Take an online course or class at a local

university to create momentum to finish the necessary require-
ments needed to make progress.

Want to move to that new city that you've dreamed about
for years? Make a plan to visit the city once a quarter and have
informational meetings with people who work in your desired
industry to start building relationships. While there, research
the housing market and neighborhoods you could one day call
home.

Putting in this effort requires a new awareness—shifting
gears, taking some risks, and not going through life at the same
speed as everyone else.

IT'S TIME TO SHIFT GEARS

If you've been used to coasting along and wearing a uniform,
even these simple examples probably sound like a lot of work
and can maybe feel overwhelming. If this is the case, I'm gonna
shoot it straight with you. It is going to be work—work that will
be worth it and that most will never do. That's why you're you
and you're reading this book. Because you're not like everyone
else. You're uncommon. Embrace that.

My invitation for you is to look at this work not as a chore
that you must do, but rather as an investment in yourself that
you *get* to do. Every single day, one step at a time, you'll have to
recommit to doing this work. As my friend Bassam Tarazi said
in his popular TEDx Talk, "You don't have to change the world.
You just have to change the moment."

Right now, take a moment and think of your life as a Ferrari. If you owned a brand-new Ferrari and only ever drove it at
thirty-five miles per hour, people would think, *What a waste of
fine Italian engineering,* as they watched drivers in Pontiac Vibes
and Chevy Bolts pass you on the freeway.

Ferraris weren't built to plod along at thirty-five miles per hour every single day. And neither were you. Ferraris were built for speed. It's time to shift gears.

We're not meant to do just-good-enough work at the office. Or pay just-okay attention to our kids, partners, and friends. We aren't programmed to shelve away our dreams for some unknown time in the future. We can't thrive if we hide who we truly are and always play it safe.

This is driving thirty-five miles per hour on the road of life when we could be accelerating. And, it's another uniform we wear to avoid having to question the status quo. What is creeping down the road with one foot on the brakes costing you? Your soul? Your happiness? Your sanity? Your integrity? Your family?

It's time to see how much you can give and stand up for something. It's time to push some buttons that need to be pushed. It's time to stop doing those things that are killing you. It's time to stop sucking in your stomach and let it hang out until you're willing to do something about it. It's time to unleash your inner "artist" and create something. It's time to stretch yourself and see how flexible you really are.

It's. Your. Time.

It's important to know that when you exceed the speed limit of life, your actions might knock others off-balance, ruffle some feathers, or make people uncomfortable. You might even get a speeding ticket. But if you never exceed the speed limit of life, your inaction will hurt you and only you.

Test your limits.

What are some shifts that you can start making today? Remember: the same actions will only get you the same results.

MY TWENTY-YEAR UNIFORM

It has taken me a long time to shift gears in my own life and it's an ongoing journey. As mentioned above, creating lasting change requires recommitting every day. Committing to something is easy. Recommitting to it every day takes courage.

Remember that blazer, the slacks, the crisp button-up shirt, and the loafers? I wore that uniform for more than just a summer. From the time of that internship in the late 1990s and over the course of my growing career up until about 2017, I kept on wearing a version of that exact uniform.

Over the years, my uniform evolved slightly. It later became the "advertising guy" or "start-up guy" or "leadership guy" look with a crisp pair of blue jeans, slim-fitting button-up shirt, dress shoes (no tassels), and designer blazer.

Then, it ended entirely.

Eventually, with each passing day and year, I found it more and more exhausting to put on the uniform—to the point where I could barely look at myself in the mirror. So, one day, I got the courage to stop wearing it.

Without my knowing it, my wardrobe had become a mask that was shielding my true feelings of dissatisfaction with an artificial definition of success. It was a persona and a layer of protection. Dressing to fit the role I was playing was creating distance between me and the rest of the world.

It was a bold move to stop wearing the uniform. I donated most of my blazers and started wearing what made me feel more like me. These days on stage, in workshops, or during coaching sessions, I wear what feels comfortable and what makes me feel happy: slacks, a crisp T-shirt, a chore jacket, and dope sneakers.

I can still remember one of the early speaking engagements I showed up to wearing this getup. I was nervous as hell. Would the client fire me on the spot because I was wearing jeans and a T-shirt instead of a button-up with a blazer?

Thankfully, that didn't happen. Interestingly, because I wasn't wearing what everyone else was wearing, I actually stood out more. After so many years of hiding in plain sight, I could actually be seen. Internally, I felt as if I commanded more respect—or maybe it was just me finally being comfortable in my own skin. These days, if I wear a blazer and button-up, it's because I want to, not because I feel like I have to.

This was around the time that I decided to ditch my reporter voice, too. (It followed me on stage as a leadership speaker.) I knew that fake, affected voice had to stop. Why? As I learned more about myself, it was too much work to keep it up. Simply put:

It's exhausting being inauthentic.

When you wear a uniform, essentially, you're playing a role not all that different from an actor. To take on the "role" requires constant energy, pretending to be someone or something you're not—constantly performing for a judgmental audience, often of your own making—and it can be draining. Even when you're not "on," it's like being in a car with the engine on, but the car is stationary, wasting valuable gasoline.

Over the years, as I've matured and become more confident in my voice and my story, I slowly but surely shed my fake voice, too. Today, when I'm on stage, I finally speak more like the guy that you'd talk to in line at a coffee shop or laugh with during a walk and talk. Odds are that when I speak, you'll hear my twang and end up asking me if I'm from down south. (No, I'm from Michigan, thank you.) It means you'll hear more slang come out of my mouth. It also means that in a casual conversation, you may even hear me throw out the occasional expletive.

Even more fascinating, if you ask me a question that I don't know the answer to, I'll actually respond, "I don't know," instead of giving you a BS answer as I used to do, trying to prove something that didn't need to be proved. More and more, I'm finding it easier to be me. It's still not exactly a breeze to always be vulnerable, but it's easier to have self-respect when I'm being real.

What does being "just you" a little bit more every day look like—in work and in life? Even if you work in an environment with a required dress code or uniform, you don't have to lose sight of the spark that drives you—and what makes you, you. In fact, holding on to that spark is essential to moving forward in life and in your career.

My advice? Be you. The good, the raw, the unpolished, and the vulnerable. Others may not fully get you, or like you, and that's okay—as long as you get you. So, go ahead and take off the uniform.

NEXT STEPS

1. What uniform(s) have you worn throughout your life? Where did you learn to wear this uniform? Was it from society, family, friends, the education system, religion, and so forth?

2. What have your uniforms provided you with? Is it money, safety, status, or security? Has your uniform served your best interests? Explain why or why not.

3. In what ways have you lived life on automatic? What's one way you could shift gears or break the speed limit of your life today?

4. Over the course of the next few days, before you speak, send a text or e-mail, or even post something on social media, pause and ask yourself: "What do I stand for? Is what I'm about to share the authentic me or is it a uniform? What do I *really* want to express?"

TURN UP THE VOLUME

"Everybody wants to be a bodybuilder,
but nobody wants to lift no heavy-ass weights."

—RONNIE COLEMAN, BODY BUILDING CHAMPION
AND FORMER MR. OLYMPIA

REMEMBER THE FAKE reporter voice I was telling you about that was part of my "uniform" for years? It all started with my first job as a local television news reporter. It was a brief experience, because after my four-week trial period at the station, I wasn't offered a job. Essentially, I was fired. You're probably thinking, *Wow, this guy gets fired a lot.* But all was not lost.

Even though at that time I had yet to find my voice—in more ways than one—I learned a powerful lesson during my short local news career that has stayed with me ever since.

One morning, I arrived at the station bright and early. The station's news director, the person responsible for hiring reporters and eventually firing me, was in his office watching something on his television. When he saw me, he waved me in.

His office was messy, filled with VHS tapes, MiniDV tapes, news scripts, and random awards. This was right around the time YouTube first launched, but still long before people were using it to send links as a way to easily watch something.

"I'm looking at reels that reporters from all across the country sent me," he said. "All of them want jobs *here*," he said, a little too proudly. He motioned for me to sit down next to him.

He put a tape into the VCR and pressed Play. It was a young female reporter. As she started talking, I couldn't hear anything. I noticed that the volume on the television was turned all the way down, but the news director didn't seem to notice.

After watching the reporter's reel for a few seconds, he ejected the tape and immediately put in another. This time is was a male reporter. Just like with the first tape, the volume was all the way down.

After about ten seconds, I had to interrupt him. "I'm sorry, but I can't hear what he's saying or what the other reporter sounded like. The volume isn't turned up."

The news director smiled proudly. It was obvious that he'd been impatiently waiting for me to say something. "I have the volume turned down on purpose."

I was confused. "How can you know if a reporter is any good if you can't hear what they're saying?"

Before answering, he paused. Then he paused some more. Finally, he said, "I want to see if I *want* to turn the volume up."

It took a second, but then his words hit me: "I want to see if I want to turn the volume up." Now that's heavy, I thought.

"Any idiot can talk into a camera and sound nice," he continued. "But it takes something special to get people to lean forward and pay attention, even when the volume is turned down. That's what I'm looking for."

This made me think about all the times that I'd been at home doing a variety of things—listening to music, ironing clothes, cooking food, or washing dishes. In the midst of all of this, the television would often be on with the volume turned down. I remembered those rare moments when something on the television would grab my attention—enough that I'd stop what I was doing, find the remote control, and turn up the volume.

It's the same way in life. Some people make you want to turn the volume up more than others. It's a lesson that I'll never forget. So, are you one of those people who make others want to turn the volume up?

PEOPLE DO JUDGE BOOKS BY THEIR COVERS

Every single day, people are deciding whether or not they want to "turn up the volume" on you and support your goals, career, or ambitions—or press Mute.

In our society, we say "Don't judge a book by its cover" so often that it's become a cliché. But the truth is, you're being judged all the damn time, whether you know it or not.

In your personal, business, or social life, people are constantly deciding whether or not they want to support you, learn more about you, and trust you—based on:

Your attitude.

The effort you give.

Your wardrobe.

Your body language.

What time you show up (by the way, if you're on time, you're late).

Your "energy," meaning: do things get better or worse when you arrive?

What a Google search of your name shows (even if it doesn't tell the whole story).

And more.

The good news? Every single day, you have the opportunity to influence this and get people to want to turn up the volume on you and to support your mission. The question is how?

WHAT DO YOU DO WHEN NO ONE IS WATCHING?

Don't worry. This section isn't about your private web browser history. It's about your effort, or lack thereof. It's about putting in the work to become the kind of person who stops people in their tracks—who makes them want to turn up the volume.

In the early 2000s, I attended a rap concert in New York City. I went to see one of my favorite artists at the time, Talib Kweli.

When the opening act hit the stage, people were still entering the venue. At first, like everyone else, I wasn't paying much attention. People were having conversations, grabbing drinks, smoking cigarettes and marijuana, or texting on their not-yet-smart phones.

That night, the audience pretty much ignored the opening act. This wasn't because their music was bad. It's just that they weren't familiar with the artist or their music. This was before YouTube, SoundCloud, and Spotify. This was when mixtapes were still made on burned CDs.

But that night, something happened that I couldn't ignore. I noticed that even though most concertgoers were ignoring the performer, it didn't seem to bother them. They still gave absolutely everything.

The performer, though not polished, was giving their all as if they were already a Grammy Award–winning artist, performing at the MTV Music Awards, or on a sold-out worldwide tour. Even though no one was watching, the artist's level of commitment made me want to turn the volume up.

After that evening, I didn't know if I'd ever hear about the opening act again. But it always stayed with me that while almost no one was watching, they gave everything. Somehow, they knew that we would hear from them again.

The question I have for you is:

What do you do when no one is watching?

Do you still give your all, or do you phone it in and just go through the motions?

It's easy to answer, "I give my all every time!" But in my experience working with clients and organizations over the years, I can tell you this isn't true most of the time. Rarely do we truly give our all. Author and retired Navy SEAL David Goggins says that when our minds tell us that we've given our all, we're really only 40 percent of the way there.

Here are a few simple examples to help you test if you're actually giving your all.

Remember those times you've been involved in group projects in the classroom or with committees at the office? Now, think about how there's *always* that one person in the group who does most of the work—*if* you let them. Do you let them do all the work while no one is watching? (Side note: If you don't know that one person who does all the work, odds are it's you.)

Another example: Say you and a friend agree to meet two times a week at 6:00 a.m. to work out together and get in better physical shape. But you receive a text message at 9:17 p.m. the night before that says, "Bad news. I can't make it to the gym tomorrow." Do you still go to the gym while no one is watching?

Maybe you're committed to eating healthily, but you're juggling a lot of responsibilities like working a job, raising a family, and volunteering at church. On a late-night ride home, when you pull into the fast-food restaurant, do you order the one "healthy" item on the menu or something that's not good for you?

What do you do when no one is watching?

Here's what I've come to learn:

What you do
when no one is watching
will determine your
success or failure in life.

Before the sprinter won the 100-meter dash at an Olympic stadium filled to capacity, she spent nearly four years training and competing while no one was in the stands.

That person who starts their own successful business and eventually leaves their full-time job? They did it by working on their entrepreneurial endeavor early in the morning before everyone was awake, and late into the night while everyone else was asleep.

The young woman attending college to become a nurse who works full time to pay her tuition each semester chips away at her goal, day by day, driven only by her dream.

These people all paved their way to success when no one was watching.

The magic happens when no one is watching.

THE ARTIST, THREE YEARS LATER

Now, let's talk again about that memorable opening act again I saw in the early 2000s. About three years after that concert, I remember hearing about some up-and-coming artist who was getting a lot of attention in the press.

I came to find out that the artist who I saw give absolutely everything while no one was watching was—wait for it—Kanye West.

It took more than three years from the time I first saw him for Kanye to emerge as a rap star. In the press, he was being called a "new artist." But the truth is, he was seasoned before he became mainstream.

It's probably fair to say that at the time, Kanye believed in Kanye. This begs the question: if Kanye didn't believe in Kanye, who would have believed in him all those nights when no one was paying attention—when rejection was the expectation, not the exception?

Call it arrogance, call it confidence, or call it conviction. But on the stage that night, one thing was clear above all else: Kanye West fundamentally believed in himself, even if this belief was driven by a fear of not succeeding. He wasn't there to ask for permission or even ask you to like his music. He expected you to. His performance demanded it. There was no hoping involved. The classic axiom holds true:

If you don't believe in yourself, good luck getting others to.

Today, people give Kanye West a hard time about his politics, his faith, and his social media diatribes. Look, I miss the old Kanye, too. And even though I don't agree with everything he says or stands for, I can't help but see him in a different light. For years, people in the industry told him to stay behind the scenes as a successful producer. But he had a different plan for himself, and he went after it.

I'm sure it would've been easy for him to phone it in all those nights that people ignored him on stage. But he didn't, and that made all the difference. He knew what very few of us figure out until it's too late: *some opportunities come only once.* And when your moment comes, you have to deliver. If you aren't prepared for this moment, it passes you by.

I know some people who, within two weeks, will stop working on a project they allegedly care about if things don't go their way. You've probably done this as well. At the end of the day, it's all about belief, dedication, and commitment.

YOU DON'T CLIMB A MOUNTAIN BY ACCIDENT

The above story illustrates something that most people forget: you don't climb a mountain by accident. It takes preparation and time. It takes dedication and effort. It takes commitment. The challenge in society today, especially with the prevalence of social media, is that everyone wants everything right now, whether or not they've earned it and have done the necessary work required while no one was watching.

People who begin brand-new jobs want a promotion or a raise three months later.

Or, people who take a beginner's improv comedy class think they're ready for *Saturday Night Live* once they complete the course.

And those people who just purchased some DJ software for their laptop and expect to rock a sold-out nightclub in Ibiza.

Look, if I could drop you off at the top of Mount Everest at 29,000 feet, what would happen? If it was a clear day, odds are you would take in an epic view, then pass out. You might even die. Why? Because your lungs haven't acclimated from a grad-ual climb, and over years of training, to very thin air. Your lungs haven't earned the altitude.

With reality TV competitions, the perception is that the winner's life is changed overnight. But is it? It's no wonder that after winning one of these competitions—whether it's singing, dancing, cooking, modeling, or glass blowing—the instant stars are often nowhere to be found just two or three years later. It's not that they're not talented. It's just that reality shows press fast-forward on what sometimes should take people years. Their success arrived prematurely. Most people have yet to put in the deep, hard work—the ten thousand hours Malcolm Gladwell writes about. They got to the top of the mountain too soon and were unable to sustain being there. It's no wonder that so many lottery winners are more likely to declare bankruptcy[1] than average Americans.

Climbing a mountain requires taking consistent steps forward in the midst of turmoil, uncertainty, setbacks, and changing conditions. It requires doing the unsexy and unglamorous work that most would rather avoid.

We have the opportunity to fall in love with the process of "climbing" and doing the work, day in and day out. More times than not, it's going to feel more like working a shift at a factory than basking in the glow of a rainbow while petting a unicorn. When you skip over key steps of doing the work, you can set yourself up for long-term problems.

Have you done the work? More importantly, are you willing to do more work? And how do you start?

A SURFING LESSON

When you live in southern California, like I do, you're pretty much guaranteed to know someone who surfs. A few of my good friends regularly surf and they absolutely love it. It's almost an addiction for them. When they talk about surfing, their eyes light up as they describe the surge of adrenaline they feel when riding a wave.

For all of this excitement, something that I find absolutely fascinating about surfing is that it's estimated that surfers spend less than 10 percent[2] of their time actually riding waves. Less than 10 percent! The way surfers talk about their sport, you'd assume they're shredding waves all day, every day. It's also easy to get this impression watching surfing highlight reels.

However, the reality is that surfers spend most of their time *not* riding waves. There's a lot of paddling, waiting, wipeouts, and even more waiting. This is, by no means, the sexy or adrenaline-fueled part of surfing, but it's necessary. After all of the paddling and waiting, when surfers finally do catch a wave, they ride it in all of its glory and bliss for just five to eight seconds. Then they paddle back out and wait for the next wave. All of that hard work for less than ten seconds of riding a wave, but surfers will tell you that it's absolutely worth it.

With surfing, all we tend to see are those highlight reels on YouTube of people riding gigantic waves. However, rarely do people talk about everything else it takes to prepare for that moment when the wave arrives and the patience that's required. Sure, they're prepared when the opportunity comes to ride a wave; they're *also* willing to wait or wipe out. It's part of the process.

TAKE ACTION ON YOUR IDEAS

We live in a society where it's become the norm to talk about doing something as opposed to actually doing it. Social media hashtags like #grinding, #hustling, and #teamnosleep have become all the rage for people sharing the alleged hard work they're putting in. Here's what I know to be true:

> **People who are truly grinding and hustling don't have time to post about hustling or grinding on social media.**

That is, of course, unless your goal is to become an Instagram influencer, which really leads to larger questions about your life aspirations that we don't have time to address in this book. But whatever your goal is, you have the opportunity to begin taking action on your ideas. Now. Today.

I guarantee that right now you have an amazing idea that's waiting for you to take action and breathe life into it. Don't let your best ideas gather dust. Every person or organization has the answers to their most complex challenges. But odds are, the answers are just sitting around somewhere never to see the light of day. Rather than striving to be an "idea person," strive to become an "I did it person."

USE THE INGREDIENTS THAT YOU HAVE

To begin taking action on your ideas, it's critical to cultivate the right mindset.

Far too many of us focus on what we don't have. We say we don't have enough money in our bank accounts, or we don't know the right people. We say we don't live in the right city or we don't have the right software on our computers.

We spend so much time identifying what we don't have that we rarely ask, "What do I have?"

Instead of waiting for the perfect moment, for the stars to align, or for Mercury retrograde to pass, I invite you to begin identifying the ingredients that you *do* have right now.

Think about a perfect meal you'd like to make. Let's say the recipe requires ten ingredients, but you only have seven of them. You can go to the grocery store and buy the remaining three ingredients. Or, you can get creative and use the seven ingredients that you *do* have to whip up a tasty meal.

In my years working as a business correspondent and journalist profiling successful companies, executives, and entrepreneurs, I learned that growth and innovation are often born from constraints.

It's not always the big organizations with large budgets, loads of resources, and a huge staff that win. Many times, it's the small, nimble, resource-strapped start-up that shakes things up and disrupts an industry. This is because they saw their circumstances (that is, their lack of ingredients) as their advantage, as opposed to their weakness. They focused on what they did have as opposed to what they didn't. Having more isn't always better.

Breakthroughs can come from constraints.

It's your job to see your constraints, your perceived limitations, as your advantage. This is how you disrupt your life for the better.

START TO IDENTIFY YOUR INGREDIENTS

According to author Jon Gordon, there are three key ingredients, or things that you can control every day: your *attitude,* the *effort* you give, and the *actions* you take. Maybe you don't have the ingredients you wish you had when it comes to your finances, relationships, health, or career. But that doesn't have to stop you from intentionally taking steps toward what you do want in each of these areas.

For your finances, this could mean getting a part-time job to earn some extra income. For your relationships, it could mean dedicating more time to those people who matter most and pruning back time from those who don't. For your health, it could look like using free online resources and apps to get your diet and exercise routine back on track. And for your career, it could mean conducting informational interviews to learn more about others and simultaneously increasing awareness about yourself.

More than anything, I'm going to ask you to incorporate pride as one of your ingredients. Not the ugly kind of pride. But the good kind of pride, where you are proud of how you show up in life. When you start and end your day, I want you to have that feeling that you played your part. You did what you said you were going to do. You didn't make excuses. You did the work when no one was watching. If for nothing else, do it for yourself. Have some pride.

Spend some dedicated time thinking about the ingredients that you do have in your life that you could be using to your advantage. Remember: don't let a couple of missing ingredients stop you from getting creative and putting in the hard work to cook up something spectacular with your life.

NEXT STEPS

1. As things are today, do people want to turn the volume up on you and support you? Explain why or why not.

2. Write down some of the times in your life when you did the work while no one was watching. What are you willing to do moving forward while no one is watching?

3. What are some ideas sitting in your notebooks, on your computer, or in your mind that you can take action on today?

4. What ingredients (resources, people, and so forth) do you have in your life that you can use to your advantage? What *do* you have available to you?

FIND YOUR EDGE

"Fear is a natural reaction to moving closer to the truth."
—PEMA CHÖDRÖN, *WHEN THINGS FALL APART*

SO, YOU'RE READY to take action with the ingredients that you've identified. You're ready to put in the work and take those important next steps to turn your big ideas for your life into a reality. What now?

Let me start with a story about one of my big ideas that I turned into a reality. In 2012, I cofounded the Ignition Lab along with my good friend, author and adventurer Bassam Tarazi.

The Ignition Lab was an accelerator where professionals who were looking to build a side hustle or business could cocreate, cosolve, and support one another.

Since a growing list of accelerators and incubators across the country had helped successful businesses and start-ups launch, we figured that based on our successful track record of coaching and facilitating workshops, we could successfully do the same for motivated professionals. The Ignition Lab was a place for them to learn, find support, and most importantly, take action with the ingredients available in their daily lives.

The target market was people who had a business idea and

wanted to dip a toe in the water to test out entrepreneurship or freelance work before jumping in completely. Or, people who were looking to transform their side hustle into something viable that could generate revenue.

Our promise was that if you applied and were accepted, we would create and facilitate a dynamic, unforgettable, six-day experience where you'd make measurable progress on the project or endeavor that mattered most to you.

Did we host this event in New York City, where Bassam lived at the time? No. Did we facilitate this in Los Angeles, where I lived? No.

Instead, we decided to host this all-inclusive, immersive, hands-on workshop for six people in the sleepy beach town of San Juan Del Sur, Nicaragua.

A few things to share before I continue:

- *Had we ever hosted an international retreat? No.*
- *Had we ever been to Nicaragua? No.*
- *Did either of us speak fluent Spanish? No.*
- *Did we secure insurance for the retreat? No.*
- *Did we work with a local event planner? No.*
- *Did our GPS work on the eighty-six-mile drive from Managua International Airport to San Juan Del Sur? No.*

Still, based on our experience, extensive planning, and preparation, we set out with an optimistic, "If anything doesn't go as planned, we'll figure it out."

Well, much of what could have gone wrong, did. We had *a lot* to figure out.

We got lost multiple times during our drive from Managua to San Juan Del Sur. The cliffside "mansion" that we rented was just a big house. It didn't have as many bedrooms as we expected so people had to share a bedroom with a stranger.

The "chef" we hired was actually just a regular cook. It turned out that selecting rappelling as an activity was a sketchy idea. The ropes that were connected to a questionable tree didn't provide much confidence as we dangled off a cliff that seemed a bit too steep for amateurs.

When a swarm of bees stung one of our participants during a group hike, based on his yelling and moaning, we wondered if he was going to die. During our surfing lesson, the one person who chose *not* to surf to avoid possible injury, and instead decided to wade and relax in the water, ended up getting stung in the foot by a stingray. We had to rush her to a local urgent care center that seemed to operate out of someone's house.

Not everything in Nicaragua went as planned. *However,* in between the few challenges that we experienced, the vast majority of things went extremely well. The Ignition Lab, and what we accomplished there with the participants, ended up being a smashing success that has generated amazing results for everyone involved. Every attendee said that it was a life-changing experience and well worth the investment they made—and beyond.

I'm sure that a fair share of people would tell us that choosing to host this event in a foreign country with so many unknowns was foolish and dangerous. Maybe it was. However, what we learned from that experience was worth its weight in gold. And looking back, I realize that what Bassam and I were doing was finding our edge.

WHAT IT MEANS TO FIND THE EDGE

Even if you don't know what finding the edge means, you know what it feels like.

If you've ever been an athlete before, do you remember that

feeling you would get before a game, match, or race began? Those butterflies in your stomach. That increased heart rate. That feeling is finding the edge.

If you've ever been a performer, like an actor, a public speaker, a musician, or a comedian, you know what it means to find the edge. That feeling you get before you take the stage, when your throat gets dry or your hands start to tremble? That feeling is finding the edge.

If you've ever had a crush on someone, you totally know what it means to find the edge. Remember that moment when your crush popped up at the right time in the right place and you finally got the courage to ask them out? Maybe your upper lip started to sweat and you felt like your heart was going to explode. That, right there, is finding the edge.

The increased heart rate, those butterflies in your stomach, the trembling hands, the dry throat—they are all signals and markers on the road. They're signs that we're getting outside of our comfort zone and putting ourselves in a position where we can stretch and grow.

Think about the last week of your life. Think about the last thirty days. When's the last time you felt any of those feelings? The heart pounding. The butterflies. That nervous energy. Those feelings that let you know that you're finding the edge.

How many times did you embark on something so challenging, or even relatively simple, that you felt your heart rate increase?

When was the last time your hands trembled in anticipation of something?

If you don't regularly feel these emotions or have these sensations, odds are that you're not growing. You're not developing. You're not moving forward. You're not stretching yourself. And that means you're standing still. Atrophy is setting in.

I once read:

If you're not close enough to the edge,
then you're taking up too much space.

This is 100 percent true. How much space are you taking up? If it's too much, it's time to find that edge again.

FEAR AND EXCITEMENT

Finding the edge is that unique place where fear and excitement meet.

During these moments, we have to decide if we're going to focus on fear and back away from something, or intentionally lean into the excitement and move forward. It's all about how we choose to approach situations and the mindset we adopt. As author and psychologist Carol Dweck writes about in her book *Mindset,* are you operating from a fixed mindset—that is, staying static—or a growth mindset, where you're continuing to grow and develop?

Many psychologists will tell you there's little physiological difference between fear and excitement. Both are aroused physiological states. But while fear shows up in our brains to protect us, excitement brings enthusiasm and motivation for taking on new things.

Psychologist Fritz Perls, founder of gestalt therapy, once said, "Fear is excitement without the breath."

Most times when we operate out of fear, our breathing is short and constricted. We're tight. But when we shift into in excitement, our lungs get all the oxygen they need and we experience what we often call "flow" or "being in the zone."

So, are you holding your breath
or are you letting it flow?

Right now, inhale deeply through your nose and fill up your lungs. Hold it for a moment. Then, release the air with a long exhale out of your mouth. Do that three times and I guarantee you'll feel more relaxed than you did a minute ago.

If you've historically approached life with fear, today is a new day. Start with a deep breath and ask yourself: "What can I be excited about?"

WHEN THE WIND IS AT YOUR BACK, JUMP

Of course, as we find the edge, important times arise when we must go beyond our feelings of fear and excitement and take notice of a true opportunity to create our own momentum. I call this having the wind at your back.

Over the years as a collegiate long and triple jumper, I was always keenly aware of the wind. If there was a headwind, I'd get extremely frustrated, knowing that a force out of my control might negatively affect the distance of my jump. However, if there was a tailwind at my back, I would feel a sense of excitement, knowing that this same force could help carry me a farther distance. A really good wind can carry you anywhere from an extra inch, to half a foot or more. It can make you feel like you are flying.

All jumpers quickly learn that:

> *You can't control which way the wind blows.*
> *But when it's at your back, you must jump.*

In my life and career, I've been cognizant of a similar feeling that crops up when I least expect it—a force that seems to propel me forward. You could say the "wind" was at my back. Here's the deal: whenever the wind blows in your favor to make a change or take action, you have to jump. This is how you create your own momentum. It's critical to jump at these moments because you never know when the wind might die down again—because eventually, it will.

So how do you know when the wind is at your back? At the risk of sounding all spiritually woo-woo (which I'm actually okay with), it's a feeling and it's an awareness. Sometimes, this feeling is tangible—you can see or feel real-life metrics (like the physical wind at your back). Other times, the wind is a feeling deep in your gut or a quiet voice that tells you things are moving in your favor. Sometimes, you can tell there's a "wind" because of the fear you might feel as you take a risk or stretch yourself. At times like these, the fear is asking you to contract. The wind is asking you to expand.

For the uninitiated, the wind can be intimidating, even frightening. Of course, it's also exciting for those very same reasons. So how do you stop yourself from second-guessing the wind? By always remembering that fear can actually be excitement with the right shift in breath, perspective, and mindset. Regularly ask yourself:

"Is this truly fear that I'm feeling? Or, is this excitement because I'm going outside of my comfort zone?"

I wish I could say that I've always jumped when the wind was at my back, but the truth is, I haven't. Sometimes, fear kept me from jumping. Other times, it was pride (the ugly kind), or a lack of faith and effort.

Over the years, not jumping with the wind has reared its head in different ways. Sometimes, it has meant not speaking my truth, passing on great career opportunities, not creating clear boundaries, missing important deadlines, not following up, not purchasing a ticket, not telling someone how I feel, not showing up, not keeping agreements, not completing a project, you name it.

I suggest that you don't allow fear to stop you from jumping. Sure, sometimes in life we can get a little overzealous with a good wind. Even greedy. However, in the end, I'd rather you jump a little too far than not jump at all. Don't forget to keep checking in with yourself—think about those last thirty days.

Here's another way to help you find the edge, jump, and assess if you're approaching life from a place of fear or excitement. Ask yourself:

"Am I living a life where I regularly contribute, or one where I regularly settle?"

Think about the last time you began a new job. Typically, a week or two in, some guy named Bob pokes his head into your office or cubicle and says with a goofy smile, "Are you all *settled* in yet?"

Our default response is to give Bob a kind smile and say something to the tune of, "I'm getting there. There's just so much to learn."

Bob smiles and says, "Don't worry. You'll get there soon enough," as he walks away to steal someone's lunch from the refrigerator in the breakroom.

As innocent as Bob's question is, and it does show compassion, it still rubs me the wrong way. In my experience, the question "Are you all settled in yet?" can sometimes translate to "Are you ready to do the exact minimum required of you to keep your job?"

My hope is that you never fully settle in, so to speak—that is, go through the motions, fall into how things "have always been done," or just check items off your list. The goal is to always be looking for ways to grow, evolve, and contribute. To regularly find the edge. To jump when the wind is at your back every single time.

FOR AS LONG AS YOU CAN

The more you contribute, the better prepared you'll be to jump at opportunities or tackle challenges when they come your way.

A few years ago, I was emceeing a major conference in Washington, D.C. More than five thousand people attended, and I was responsible for steering the ship from a high-tech stage, keeping the audience engaged, and making the event run smoothly. One of the speakers at this conference was the Vice President of the United States.

After introducing a video to the audience, I remember walking backstage. The executive producer of the conference production team immediately came up to me and informed me that the Vice President was running behind schedule. This added a major hiccup to the production schedule, because we couldn't put another big-name speaker on stage until after the Vice President spoke.

"Antonio, after this video finishes, I need to you stall and entertain the audience," the executive producer said to me.

Even though this wasn't my first rodeo, I was still caught off guard. I had experienced this kind of thing in television, but rarely with my public-speaking work. In television, you could always play a commercial, but this was different. "How long do you need me to stall?" I asked.

He looked me directly in the eyes, like a doctor breaking bad news to a patient. He sighed and then said, "For as long as you can."

Normally this wouldn't be a problem. But this was one of

the few events where I wasn't a speaker delivering a one-hour keynote. My job at this conference was supposed to involve serving as emcee, reading a teleprompter, announcing speakers, interviewing guests of honor, and providing logistical information. Essentially, I had turned off the speaker side of my brain. Now I needed to stall for as long as I could.

I looked at the executive producer and said with as much confidence as I could muster, "I got you."

As I turned around and walked back toward the curtain on the stage—where I'd soon be in front of five thousand people with no plan—I thought, *What the hell am I going to do?*

I was about to find the edge and experience what I call a "red-light moment."

RED-LIGHT MOMENTS

During my television career, I often found myself in a television studio standing on an *X* marked by black tape on the floor, bright lights shining on me.

I was surrounded by a production crew and sometimes a studio audience. There'd be large television cameras pointed at me, too.

The stage manager would say loud enough for everyone to hear, "We're going live in five seconds." In my mind, I'd be excitedly thinking, *Wow, in five seconds, I'll be on live television, broadcasting to millions of people all across the country.*

"Five, four . . ." The stage manager would begin his countdown.

Then, like clockwork—or like the devil showing up—my mind would quickly shift to fear mode. *Millions of people. Oh no. That's a lot of people,* I would think. I would slowly start to panic. I shifted from excitement to fear.

"Three . . . two . . . one," the stage manager would continue, and then point at me.

A red light on top of the camera flashed on. We were now broadcasting live. That was my cue to read the words off the teleprompter or recite the lines I had memorized.

Instead, I froze. In those moments, I was a deer in headlights. I could feel the studio audience and production staff staring at me with that "oh no" look in their eyes. In those moments, I knew I had to make a choice to fly or fall flat on my face in front of millions.

Early on in my career, I regularly experienced this overwhelming panic. And when I started public speaking, I experienced the same thing on stages in front of crowds with hundreds or thousands of people.

These red-light moments present us with the chance to make a potentially life-changing, confidence-building decision. They are the critical points when we're faced with a choice: to act, or not act. To bet on ourselves, or not.

These moments push us into new territory. When we take meaningful risks, that's when we create our own luck and build momentum in our lives.

Chances are you've experienced red-light moments of your own. Early in our lives, we encounter plenty of these opportunities when:

- *Asking our crush out on a date.*

- *Studying abroad in college.*

- *Joining a band.*

- *Moving to a new city.*

- *Changing industries early on in our careers.*

- *Starting that business in a garage.*

- *Doing the opposite of what our parents want us to do.*

- *Pursuing our art, even though people tell us to get a "real job."*

- *Taking a year off to travel the world when people say we're supposed to be full-on adulting.*

- *Joining the Peace Corps or teaching English as a second language in a developing country.*

Interestingly enough, I have found that the older we get, the less we encounter red-light moments. This is because we wait too long. We get too comfortable. We stay for that one last bonus at work. We fail to leave a relationship that brings us no joy because we're afraid of being alone.

Or, we no longer encounter red-light moments because we start to accumulate so much stuff—mortgages, car payments, charcuterie boards—that we become paralyzed. Our decisions and increased responsibilities become repellent to our red-light moments. It can even get to the point where we fail to recognize red-light moments as opportunities that can have a profound effect on our lives. Here's what you must know:

Your dreams need encouragement at any age.

Your dreams need your action. Your dreams need you to do the work that's required. Your dreams need you, no matter how busy your life may seem. We must create more red-light moments and develop a plan of attack to seize those moments when they arise.

Seeking out red-light moments doesn't always mean that things will work out. What it means is that we're finding the edge, being active, contributing, and taking the reins of our lives into our own hands.

HOW TO FIND YOUR EDGE

Finding the edge means being willing to regularly, even deliberately, feel uncomfortable—to push yourself to the edge of what you already know you can do.

Finding the edge can be as simple or as challenging as taking a public-speaking class or finally booking that trip abroad.

It can mean going to dinner by yourself at the new restaurant instead of pulling teeth trying to get someone to join you.

Finding the edge can be introducing yourself to that stranger next to you on the plane who could be your future business partner or spouse.

It can mean saying yes to the invitation to join coworkers at happy hour, even though you don't know them very well.

Finding the edge can mean having that tough conversation with your boss that could finally move your career forward.

Maybe it's pressing Publish on a blog post.

Or, it could be apologizing to someone you hurt or let down.

When you find your edge, it reminds you that you're alive. That you're living actively, rather than passively. You have the ultimate say in what happens in your life.

Remember: if you don't regularly find *your* edge, odds are you aren't growing, developing, and moving forward in life. Of course, it must be noted that there's a big difference between going to the edge and falling off the edge. Awareness, discernment, and surrounding yourself with the right people (as you'll learn in the next chapter) are all critical.

The edge is where the magic happens—not sitting on the couch binging on Netflix, no matter how safe and comfortable that might feel.

When was the last time *you* found the edge? Has it been longer than you care to admit?

CONFIDENCE IS EARNED

When it comes to life, many fail to realize that breakthroughs often come in small steps. You don't have to host a retreat in Nicaragua or speak off the cuff in front of five thousand people to find the edge. Too many are trying to jump the Grand Canyon when they should instead start with a puddle.

People think they have to take a big leap to accomplish their goals or move forward. But it's actually a series of small actions. Sometimes it starts with just figuring out the next single step to take, instead of trying to map out the next five. Taking one step in the right direction is better than standing still or not moving at all.

If you have an axe and you want to chop down a large oak tree, the first swing won't do much. Nor will the second, third, or fourth. But with consistency and dedication, eventually, that tree will come down.

In all facets of your life, ask yourself, "How can I chip away at this just a little today?" Every day, just take one swing or one step.

Most people aren't patient enough to stick it out till the tree falls down. Maybe on some level, they don't know how because they've never been responsible for seeing something through to the end.

Well, today is a new day, my friend. With dedication, commitment, and consistency, you'll experience minibreakthroughs— sometimes ones we can't even imagine yet. This works like compound interest and can lead to exponential growth, even if you start small. You just have to keep making deposits. Slowly, you'll build up your confidence and become the kind of person who regularly experiences breakthroughs.

That's what ended up happening at that conference in Washington, D.C. when we were waiting for the Vice President. "For as long as you can" ended up being only about fifteen minutes.

By going through the Rolodex of stories in my brain, short excerpts from my keynote speeches, and a few videos that I had available for emergencies, it all worked out. I was a professional. I did what I was paid to do. I found the edge in real time. It was simultaneously nerve-racking and exhilarating.

People always say you have to shoot your shot and take chances. I agree. And, I invite you to shoot your shot more often. Seize on opportunities to show the world what you've got and do what you do best. That's how you create your own luck.

A FINAL NOTE ON FINDING THE EDGE

When you regularly find the edge and push yourself beyond the limits that you're used to, sometimes you can find yourself feeling a bit of a letdown afterward. Don't worry, this is completely normal. I like to call this energy shift "earned sadness."

Earned sadness is what you feel when something comes to an end because it challenged or stretched you like never before. It could have even been a profound life-changing experience or a project that took some time to complete.

It's like when kids go off to summer camp. Most times, they're afraid to leave their parents, siblings, and home. However, when their parents return to pick them up in a couple of weeks, although they're happy to see mom and dad, they're also sad to have the experience come to an end and leave behind the new friends and amazing experiences they collected. They're different people than they were just a couple of weeks before.

This feeling of sadness, when a meaningful experience comes to end, means that you've done something right. It means that you're finding the edge and that you're jumping.

NEXT STEPS

1. Think about and describe times in your life when you found the edge and when you jumped when the wind was at your back. What did it look and feel like?

2. Historically, how have you approached life—with a fear- or excitement-based mindset? Are you currently settling in life or actively contributing?

3. Describe a red-light moment from your life when you had to make a real-time decision. How did it play out?

4. List one to three ways you can find your edge, little by little:

    - *Daily* (e.g., new sports/exercise classes; new responsibilities at work)

    - *Weekly* (e.g., professional classes; going on a certain number of dates)

    - *Monthly* (e.g., giving talks at work or conferences; volunteering)

    - *Yearly* (e.g., taking an exciting vacation; performing in that orchestra or play)

BUILD YOUR TEAM

"A man only learns in two ways, one by reading,
and the other by association with smarter people."

—WILL ROGERS, ACTOR, COWBOY, AND HUMORIST

FOR NEARLY THE past five years, every Thursday morning when I'm not on the road, I meet with the same group of guys at 7:00 a.m. We call it Man Morning.

This group is as diverse as they come—with men from different professions, backgrounds, and ages. Some are married, others are single. Some have kids, others don't. Some run their own businesses, others work for companies.

For an hour we turn off our phones, head out for a hike, and discuss everything from relationships to business to personal finances. No topic is off-limits.

Based on our established ground rules, during our weekly hikes we listen without judgment. Instead of offering solutions, everyone asks great questions to help you rethink or reframe whatever you're experiencing. We hold each other accountable, even if the feedback is tough to hear. Everything is confidential among members of the group.

What the Man Morning crew has in common is a commitment to supporting one another through ups, downs, and everything in between. We knew that if we did this over cocktails in the evening, it wouldn't be nearly as powerful. We knew this because we tried. Talking over drinks at the end of the day at a bar proved to be very different from our open-air nature sessions first thing in the morning. Alcohol shifted the intention and vibes of our conversations. Sure, the drinks were fun, but rarely did we talk about what really needed to be addressed.

The great thing about Man Morning is that you can't hide behind social media posts, text messages, or "I'm crazy busy" excuses. At Man Morning, people look you in the eye. They hold you to your own real-life standards and you're expected to contribute.

Before Man Morning, whenever I found myself feeling stuck, lost, or in a funk, I'd often retreat from family and friends. Something felt safe about isolation in the midst of fear and uncertainty. This is true for others, too.

Studies find that loneliness is at epidemic levels[1] in the United States—so much so that is was declared a public health crisis.[2] In fact, one out of five Americans[3] say they have no one to talk to when they're going through a tough time.

With my commitment to Man Morning, loneliness and isolation are no longer options. This group of men has guided me through rough patches and challenging times as I navigated my marriage, family, and business life. I don't just look forward to these meetups—I need them. They've made me a better person. Along the way, I've also become happier, earned more income, matured into being a better husband and father, and made positive changes that impact my health.

I've also learned that it's not solely about other people supporting my dreams. It's equally important and powerful to help others. During these moments we learn something not so surprising:

Personal breakthroughs can happen when we're helping others.

To be bold again, make progress, and ensure that your best days are ahead of you, you need a team. You don't have to fly solo and figure everything out on your own. As you've probably heard throughout your life, you are who you surround yourself with. And it's never too late to surround yourself with great people.

No one who has accomplished anything of significance did it alone. Neither should you.

WHO MAKES YOU BETTER?

Growing up, track and field was my favorite sport. Every four years, I'd sit glued to the TV watching Olympic events like sprints, relay races, high jumps, long jumps, you name it. I can still remember watching Carl Lewis win four gold medals at the 1984 Los Angeles Olympics. It was my dream to compete in the Olympics, too.

Though I eventually realized that I didn't have the talent to compete with the best athletes in the world, when I was a freshman undergrad at Western Michigan University, I tried out for the track and field team. I was good enough to earn a spot on the roster as a "walk-on" triple jumper.

In NCAA sports, a walk-on is someone who tried out for the team and made the roster but didn't earn a scholarship. My spot on the team wasn't guaranteed, and I was in the precarious position of having to compete for my place on the roster every day. At any point, I could get cut from the team.

Even though I thought I was working hard, after two years of competing on the team, I wasn't doing great. I knew that because one day, my head coach, Jack Shaw—an imposing man in his late fifties with slicked-back hair and bifocal glasses— came up to me on the track and said, "Neves, you're doing absolutely horrible."

Coach Shaw never missed an opportunity to teach a lesson with some expletive-filled straight talk. He would share memorable, though unknown proverbs, like: "Saying and doing is like farting and screwing." Or, one of my favorites: "If you aren't running fast enough, then just turn right and get off the track." Though I couldn't fully appreciate him at the time, I was fortunate to have Coach Shaw in my life. The day he told me that I was doing horrible, I thought it would be my last day with the team.

In those first two years on the team, I only ever placed first in the line at McDonald's after our competitions. The agreement Coach Shaw and I had made was that if I placed in major competitions, I'd have the opportunity to earn a partial scholarship to help pay for my tuition. Any amount of money would have helped because my single mother was paying a portion of my tuition on her credit card.

But there I was, performing like crap and hanging on for dear life. I hadn't even come close to placing in a major competition. The day that Coach Shaw told me I was doing horrible, he also shared a lesson with me that I'd never forget.

"I don't know if you know this, but we have two all-Americans on our team," he said, pointing to two of my teammates working out on the track. In collegiate sports, all-Americans are the best of the best and voted the top athletes in the country. One of these all-Americans would go on to compete in the Olympics, and the other the World Athletics Championships.

"In your two years on the team, I've never seen you work out or spend time with either of them," he continued. "Instead, you're spending your time with those guys," and he pointed to a group of my teammates who were lying back on the high-jump mat, laughing and having a good time. These guys weren't losers, but they also weren't all-Americans.

I waited for Coach Shaw to say more. However, he just looked at me with a combination of disappointment, disdain, and the unsaid message that I was letting him down. It wasn't until years later that I realized I wasn't letting him down—I was actually letting *myself* down.

Coach Shaw was absolutely right. I didn't spend time with the two all-Americans. Why? Because they got up earlier than I did. They ate better than I did. They did more repetitions in the weight room than I did. All of the parties I went to, they avoided.

In short, they were everything I was not and everything I was unwilling to be. They had the discipline, focus, and commitment required to compete at the top level of collegiate sports. They wouldn't accept mediocrity. God forbid, I exert some effort to see if I could unleash the same potential inside of me.

But spending time with teammates who joked around and relaxed on the high-jump mat was easy. With them, I could go through the motions at practice. If I gave a less-than-stellar effort (which was the norm), no one questioned me. But as much as I loved spending time with these guys, they didn't make me better.

This experience with Coach Shaw left me asking myself: *Who makes me better?*

FIND YOUR ALLIES

The concept of "who makes you better" exists beyond sports. This theme plays a vital role in all of our lives, careers, and relationships. At its core, it's about taking a close look at who we *choose* to surround ourselves with and who we set boundaries with. I emphasize *choose* because it's an active choice we make and control.

When it comes to identifying *who makes us better,* we're making a choice between spending time with what I like to call "Allies of Glory" or "Thieves of Ambition."

Thieves of Ambition are people who:

- *Do not encourage you.*
- *Do not inspire you.*

- *Do not challenge you.*

- *Do not push you.*

- *Do not hold you accountable to be the absolute best version of yourself.*

Thieves of Ambition leave you with less energy than you had before you spent time with them. They suck the life out of a room and make everyone around them feel lethargic.

Thieves take up your time talking about all the things that they're going to do, knowing they're never going to do them.

Thieves always have drama going on in their lives. When you call them, the first thing they say is, "You're not going to believe what just happened to me!" This refrain has become so routine that you want to scream back, "Why are things always happening to *you* and no one else?"

Thieves call others out on their behavior but do nothing more.

On the flip side, Allies of Glory are people who:

- *Encourage you.*

- *Inspire you.*

- *Challenge you.*

- *Push you.*

- *Hold you accountable to be the absolute best version of yourself.*

Allies of Glory bring positivity into the room. After you spend time with them, you have more energy and can feel the blood pumping through your veins.

Allies are excited to hear about what you want to accomplish, and they actually help you get started and create momentum.

Instead of having drama in their lives, allies have great things going on.

Instead of conveniently calling someone out for their behavior, allies call each other *up*. Even if it's with tough love, like Coach Shaw did with me.

If you haven't already figured it out, you want Allies of Glory in your life.

I'm going to invite you to think about the people you spend the most time with. Visualize each one of them one by one. Now, here's a hard, yet simple, question:

Do the five people you spend the most time with make you better?

YOU PAY FOR THE RED INK

Of course, the people who make you better might also challenge you in unexpected and even uncomfortable ways. When I began as a graduate student at Columbia University, I remember submitting assignments to my professors with dread. Whether it was an article that I'd spent weeks reporting on, or a script that I'd labored over for a weekly news broadcast, I pretty much knew what to expect:

Red ink. Lots of red ink.

Without fail, no matter how polished I thought my story was, the assignment would come back filled with red ink highlighting errors, missed opportunities, and questions that needed to be answered. Now and then, the red ink would include instructions to start over.

At times, throwing in the towel seemed a whole lot more

appealing than trying to fix every one of those details. And so, I'd react defensively and challenge my professors on almost every ounce of red ink they'd spilled onto my paper.

I remember complaining to friends—or anyone who would listen. I mean, what did my professors know anyway? (Spoken like a twenty-something who wasn't wise enough to know how much he didn't know.)

Not surprisingly, the faculty at the Columbia University Journalism School is top-notch. Walking the halls are Pulitzer Prize winners, duPont-Columbia Award winners, Emmy Award winners, and more. These preeminent leaders in their fields were the same men and women investing time to help students become exceptional journalists.

What I needed wasn't better professors—it was a shift in perspective.

One day, when a Pulitzer Prize–winning professor saw how dejected I was from his red ink, he pulled me aside and said something I'll never forget: "Don't you know that you pay for the red ink?" (Because yes, I was paying ridiculously high Ivy League tuition.)

After this exchange, I realized I had two options. I could spend my time at the most respected journalism school in the world being defensive and closed-minded. Or, I could do what I was there to do—learn. Of course, this required me to accept a painful truth. My writing and reporting needed serious work. So did my ego.

Eventually, I actually learned to appreciate the red ink. Why? Because it meant that I had an opportunity to improve—to develop, to grow, to stretch myself—all under the guidance of a master.

With time (and lots of red ink), my writing improved. I learned more than I could've imagined during my time in graduate school. But nothing has proven more valuable than learning how to be edited, or in other words, how to take constructive criticism.

Unbeknownst to me at the time, my professor was being a true ally to me, simultaneously challenging and encouraging me to improve and put in the necessary work. This means going above and beyond what's required as opposed to cutting corners and doing just-good-enough work. It means being willing to do the work when no one is watching as explained in chapter eight. And, it means pushing ourselves to our limits so we can find the edge and grow instead of settling for the status quo.

VULNERABILITY ISN'T OPTIONAL

Learning to be edited and critiqued in a constructive way isn't easy. It requires being open-minded, humble, and most of all, vulnerable.

As a coach, I've facilitated my share of masterminds where the participants fundamentally understood the importance of getting this kind of feedback. (Masterminds are a group of people who come together to support each other on existing or new endeavors. In other words, they're a group of allies.)

One of my most memorable experiences was facilitating a group of successful serial entrepreneurs at a rented home in Venice, California. All of their résumés, track records, and backgrounds were equally impressive. Most had built companies that generated millions of dollars in revenue or had been part of companies that had sold for millions of dollars.

What these entrepreneurs all had in common was that they were working on new endeavors and wanted to receive feedback and advice from people they trusted. At this point in their careers, they could've been traveling the world and relaxing—doing anything but participating in this mastermind session—but that's not how they were wired.

Sure, over the course of three days we did activities like yoga and surfing, and ate meals prepared by a private chef. Still, they weren't afraid to do the hard work. They each presented and debated the merits of their new business ideas.

But this is what really stayed with me. Each time one of these entrepreneurs—people who were already very successful in the eyes of their peers—got up to present their new business idea, you could see the fear and vulnerability in their eyes. They were putting themselves out there, finding the edge, and they were open to receiving real criticism and feedback.

And yes, sometimes this real-time feedback was tough to digest, especially when it involved concerns about their new endeavor. But at the end of their sessions, over dinner when the feedback was on pause, there was no doubt how thankful they were to get something many of us tend to avoid. What they were receiving was good friction. They were being called up.

FIND GOOD FRICTION

Where I was raised in Michigan, it snows a lot. This means that every now and then, you might find yourself stuck in your car. Your tires may be spinning nonstop, but you're not going anywhere because the tread can't find traction on the snow and ice.

If you've ever found yourself in this situation, you know you have a few options to get unstuck. You can put something like sand, salt, or kitty litter under your tires. These cause enough friction on the tread to propel you forward.

If you're striving to make progress
on anything meaningful in your life,
what you need most is good friction.

What is good friction, exactly? It's another way to describe getting real, constructive feedback that holds us accountable. It helps us find our footing so we can get traction. It pushes us to be a little better in our work and everyday lives.

Good friction calls others *up* to be better versions of themselves. Bad friction calls others *out*. Growth is rarely a byproduct of calling someone out—that's called shaming. Good friction refuels you as opposed to draining you.

Think of the last time someone gave you feedback, solicited or not, on a project you worked hard on or care about deeply. Whether the feedback came from your boss at work or from a long-trusted friend, if you're like most people, chances are you first heard the feedback as criticism. Maybe you even got defensive and thought, *What does he know anyway? What an idiot, I should cancel him.*

Sharing your work with others—whether it is a blog post, a work project you busted your butt on, a piece of jewelry you made at your kitchen table, or a novel you've been toiling away at for years—is inherently vulnerable. Even for the most confident among us, finding and dealing with good friction can be challenging. How do you get pushed just hard enough outside your comfort zone without being knocked flat on your back?

Getting real, honest feedback doesn't have to cut like a knife. When you find yourself receiving good friction from someone, remind yourself of these important lessons:

Growth comes from good friction. Regularly ask yourself, "How will this friction improve my project or endeavor and push me farther than I've gone before?" The simple act of asking this question opens us up to true growth and development, even if what we hear isn't easy to digest.

Top performers don't avoid good friction. Instead, they seek it out. If you have the opportunity to get constructive criticism from a trusted source, accept it.

Breakthroughs come from good friction. Progress can only happen when we stop cloistering the projects and things that matter most to us and open them up to good friction.

In all that you do, I encourage you to seek more good friction. Create a feedback mechanism for all the projects that matter most to you. Don't forget that you get to choose if you're going to accept, or dismiss, the feedback you receive.

IDENTIFYING YOUR ALLIES AND THIEVES

Let's revisit a couple of questions posed earlier in this chapter. *Do the people you spend the most time with make you better? Are you spending time with allies or thieves?*

Odds are that you've heard a version of this Jim Rohn quote: "Show me your five closest friends and I'll show you your future."

Today in the twenty-first century, it should be: "Show me the people you spend time with in real life, not just on technology, and I'll show you your future."

The research backs me up on this. According to a study from the London School of Economics,[4] a major component of happiness is having rich social bonds and meaningful relationships in your life.

As much as I love digital learning and social media to stay connected with friends, one thing remains clear:

Real-life relationships are more powerful than digital ones.

Don't let anyone tell you otherwise.

Digital friendships, where you communicate primarily via technology, don't come close to offering the value that in-person ones do. As an example, if you take an online class and an in-person version of the same class, chances are the in-person class will be one hundred times better, based on the real-time human interactions and dynamics at play.

Once again, think about the people you spend the most time with. Now, write their names down in a notebook and answer this question:

Do they make you better?

Be brutally honest with yourself. Next to each name, actually write *yes* or *no*.

Do these people give you time and energy to make you better and help you move forward? Or, do they hurt your progress, keeping you in exactly the same place as you were yesterday and complaining about the same stuff?

As you look at your list, it may be hard to acknowledge the names of people who *don't* make you better. Especially if you've known them a long time. More than likely, they're not necessarily bad people—but they're also not playing an active role in supporting and encouraging you to achieve your goals.

Some of these people might be new in your life and you spend time with them out of convenience. Others, you've known for years—from childhood, college, or previous jobs. And here's the tough one: some might be family.

With this new vocabulary, what I don't want you to do is to start calling people out with text messages, social media posts, or direct messages that say: "Brenda, you are a thief of ambition! Begone from my life this instant."

Everything you're learning simply creates awareness to help you make better decisions. Sure, more than likely this means you will eventually have to create boundaries or spend less time with certain people, but it's all for your greater good.

Getting the results we crave sometimes means learning to let go of people who work against our best interests.

BUILDING YOUR TEAM OF ALLIES

Now this is where it gets fun. Review the names on your list that you wrote a *yes* next to. These are your current allies.

If you don't have many, or this list is a struggle, that's okay. It's time to start cultivating your team or what I like to call your personal board of advisors.

So, what does a team of allies look like?

Your team is what a board of directors is to an organization—a small but important group of people that guides decision making, provides critical input and advice, and meets with you on a regular basis, either individually or as a group.

Believe it or not, these people are already in your network. It's just your job to identify them and to stay in regular contact with them, sharing updates, developments, thank-yous, setbacks, and achievements. This is how you get them vested in your success.

If you don't see the power of having allies in your life, here's why it's so important. There's a reason top CEOs, executives, entrepreneurs, and athletes work with coaches: objectivity. Allies can see from an objective and unbiased point of view what you're likely to miss. Often, our family and friends can't play this role for us because they're too close and anything but objective.

When it comes to finding the right allies, look for a combination of well-lived expertise and experience. If you select your allies carefully, many of them will have been there, done that on issues that matter to you. Others will be hungry and happy like you, eager to start making things happen.

To be clear, allies don't necessarily have to be people you consider friends—but they can be. Sure, the relationships may evolve into friendships, but many of your allies may begin as mentors, colleagues, friends of friends, coaches that you pay, professors, pastors, and beyond.

To determine who should be on your team, review your notes from chapter 6, "What Do You Want?" Identify three to five key areas where you need support. This could be improving your marriage, changing your career, building a new business, getting out of debt, or doing something else that matters to you.

If the idea of what you want in your life is still vague and this is a struggle, you can always just identify positive people who are up to good things, whom you'd like to learn from and spend time with.

Okay. Now that you've identified where you need support, it's time to start building your team of allies. I recommend having at least five allies in your life. You may not meet up with them all together or as frequently as I get together with my Man Morning crew, and they may not even know each other. That's just fine.

Remember, allies are the people with a unique set of skills and expertise who encourage you, inspire you, empower you, challenge you, and push you to be the absolute best version of yourself.

A good way to look at these men and women is like the starting five of a basketball team. Each ally has a unique role to play. Here are the key types of people I've found to work as perfect allies:

The Encourager. *This ally does the work that many don't see. But when they're around, you always seem to be at your best. During tough spells, they support you with perspective and their unwavering commitment.*

The Playmaker. *This ally is often in the midst of making great things happen. When you need a jolt of creativity, energy, or motivation, they are your person. They move fast and don't have patience for indecision. They remind you that if you miss a shot, just keep shooting.*

The Facilitator. *This ally sees the big picture and supports you in managing the flow of information. They're good at knowing when you can speed things up or slow things down. In short, they can see things that you can't. They're a great connector and provide sound guidance.*

The Rock. *This ally is the veteran. When all hell is breaking loose, they help you remember what's most important and provide you with perspective. You need them to keep you grounded and supported while they provide valuable alignment and vision related to your goals.*

The Bruiser. *A bruiser holds you accountable for what you said you were going to do. If you tell them you're writing a book, they'll ask questions like "When will it be finished?" They are metrics-based and measure success by the progress you do or don't make.*

Once again, it's important to remember that your allies aren't always going to be your best friends. You probably won't talk to them daily. But when it's time to play ball, they'll bring out the best in you every time.

Don't be afraid to work with the best.

If you're trying to write a book or a screenplay, set up a writers' club meetup. If you're looking to grow your business, find your own mastermind feedback group. If you're navigating a transition in your life, professional or otherwise, consider working with an experienced coach every other week or join a group coaching program. If your goal is to run a marathon, train with runners who push you to run smarter and better.

Create opportunities to meet up with your allies on a regular basis. Surround yourself with greatness as much as you can.

DO YOU MAKE OTHERS BETTER?

Now let's turn the ally question around for a moment. It's also important to ask ourselves, "Are we being thieves or allies to other people in our lives?"

To be clear, being a thief doesn't have to be as dramatic as it sounds. I'm not talking about people who rob banks, commit crimes, or steal office supplies. It can be a lot less innocuous.

For example, let's say you're grabbing a beer with a friend after work. After one drink, your friend says, "It was great meeting up. I'm going to head home. There's a project I want to finish tonight."

When you respond with some subtle peer pressure, "Come on. Have just one more," you're being a thief. Your seemingly innocent comment could keep them from doing something that's important to them. It's your job to be a better ally to others, too. After all, you get what you give.

When I think back on my life, I've had different thieves and allies at every stage. When I was on that track and field team in college, identifying my Allies of Glory and Thieves of Ambition wasn't all that difficult. Coach Shaw made that clear.

In that case, in just under a year of spending more time with and observing my Allies of Glory, I experienced results that had previously eluded me. No, I never got close to the Olympics or the NCAA championships. What I did accomplish was knowing what it felt like to give my all and to surround myself with people who made me better. Though I never captured a conference championship, I learned what it took to be a champion. I did go on to become an all-conference triple jumper. Along the way, I earned the respect of my teammates, coaches, and most important, myself. And I earned that partial scholarship (all one thousand dollars of it), which meant my mother no longer had to pay for a portion of my tuition on her credit card.

From these valuable experiences, I learned two lessons: First, we aren't meant to fly solo and figure everything out on our own. Second, it's never too late to surround ourselves with good people. Get started today with identifying your allies and building your team.

NEXT STEPS

1. Identify the five people you spend the most time with. Are they allies or thieves? Why?

2. Create a list of five people who you know would add positive value to your life. Identify what's unique and special about them.

3. Do you regularly experience "red ink," or good friction? What areas in your life could benefit from receiving this kind of constructive feedback?

4. How can you be a better ally and work to make the people who are important to you better?

11

BE YOUR OWN BENEFACTOR

*"I have learned this . . . that if one advances confidently
in the direction of his dreams, and endeavors to live
the life which he has imagined, he will meet with
a success unexpected in common hours."*

—HENRY DAVID THOREAU

WHEN I ANNOUNCED to family, friends, and colleagues that I was leaving the television industry behind in New York City and moving to Los Angeles to pursue leadership and development work, some of the responses I received caught me off guard.

"You're making a horrible decision," one person told me.

"You're contracted with a major television network. Who in the hell would leave that to become a *life* coach?" another person said, with extra emphasis on the word *life*.

A thoughtful friend of mine said, "So, this is a creative way of saying that you want to be unemployed."

At the time, I didn't feel like I was surrounded by many allies. Maybe this is because I was deciding to go in a new direction with my life, one that was uncertain—and uncertainty makes our peers, and even society, uncomfortable. But here's the thing: very few people asked me *why* I was making this decision or why I wanted to leave the television industry behind. If they had asked, I would've told them that I'd pursued a career in TV for all of the wrong reasons.

For as long as I could remember, I had craved external validation, although at times I was unaware that this was driving my actions and decision making. Working in the TV industry was my uniform. More personally, I would've told them that after ten-plus years, New York City no longer felt like home. I was ready to say goodbye to all of that. Finally, I would've told them how much I loved coaching, public speaking, and helping people develop their careers and lives.

One of the most unfortunate by-products of personal growth is that the new path we choose for ourselves can sometimes create distance and negative friction with people we care about most.

To put it bluntly:

What makes you happy can make other people uncomfortable.

IT THREATENS PEOPLE WHEN YOU GROW

As you begin to evolve and grow—spending time with allies or changing your surroundings—you may find yourself experiencing resistance from some of the people who know you best.

More than likely, it will start with subtle statements like:

"You've changed . . ."

"I remember when you used to . . ."

"You never would've done that before . . ."

Of course, you want to respond, "Yes, I *have* changed! You wanted me to stay the same?" In my experience, as you stretch yourself and do something positive in your life, you'll sometimes encounter a passive-aggressive tension between you and those around you who aren't also positively evolving in their lives.

For example, let's say that you're starting to make progress on your goals to lose weight, eat healthy, and work out more. As you start to see real, tangible results, it may seem like friends or family will start showing up out of the blue with desserts or the fast food that you're working hard to avoid.

Or, say you've decided to step it up at your job and deliver above-average work. As you go above and beyond and begin to add tangible value and get recognized by management, colleagues may say things like, "Chill out, you're making the rest of us look bad," or tease you for working so hard.

It can be challenging to make sense of all of this. What you know is that it doesn't feel good. In fact, it's frustrating as hell. This is sabotage, shaming, or bullying, intentional or not, from people who say they care about us.

Why does this happen? Why do haters, saboteurs, nonbelievers, and even our family and friends show up with daggers when we actually need their support the most? The answer is simple and not so simple. The hard truth is *your growth threatens them*.

That's because the forward momentum that you're experiencing can make those around you feel like they're being left behind in your dust. Your progress and boldness can hold up a full-length mirror to what others are *not* doing in their own lives. Your success causes them (and I'm sorry for this) to project their insecurities and fears onto you.

Sometimes your family and friends won't understand or accept the choices you make.

At times, those closest to you may even attempt to make you feel guilty or give you a hard time. Of course, you'll hear things like "I just want what's best for you."

Be wary when you hear this, because "I just want what's best for you" can translate to: "I want you to stay exactly where you are in life so it's easier for me to be fine with being unhappy in my own life and refusing to make any tough changes."

Boom.

The next time someone says, "I just want what's best for you," ask yourself if they actually want what's best for you or for them. Don't allow their immaturity and lack of consciousness to change the trajectory of the life that you're working so hard to build.

On a side note, always remember that the right people will be inspired, not scared or intimidated, by your growth.

> *Surround yourself with people*
> *who are excited to see you win.*

SUPPORT IS NOT GUARANTEED

Now here's another surprising truth. During my many periods of stretching myself and growing and all of the ups and downs that came with this, I learned something profound:

> *Sometimes, the people who support you the most*
> *know you the least.*

As you pursue your dreams, you'll find that it's not always friends or family who will gladly open doors for you. This doesn't have to be a sad thing. Viewed through the right lens, this can be a beautiful thing about humanity: that a person you barely know—the stranger you met on a plane, the person you sit next to at church, or someone you connected with on social media—can help you, and wants to help you, in meaningful ways.

This is something I experienced firsthand when I started doing leadership and development work. Some of the friends and colleagues who I'd assumed would make introductions or refer me to projects, instead provided me with excuses about bad timing—or worse, ignored my calls and e-mails. Did they owe me anything? Absolutely not. Did I still naïvely think they would have my back? Yes.

Thankfully, other people pleasantly surprised me by being super generous with their time, referrals, and support. They helped me jump-start my business and reboot my life.

But not everyone will support your growth. Not everyone will agree with the decisions that you make. Not everyone will root for your success as much as you thought they would. Not everyone will join you in your next chapter.

As tough as this is to digest, it's simply one of life's bitter pills that we must swallow. However, don't let anyone's lack of support hold you back. Never forget:

> *Just because you're going your own way, doesn't mean it's the wrong way.*

ENDORSE YOURSELF

As you start to branch off in a new direction, you'll notice a shift. If you're used to following the crowd and doing what's expected of you, it can be jarring to stand alone as you pursue something that might put you at odds with others.

This new stand can be scary. You might find yourself facing inner turmoil and resistance because humans are social animals—we seek commonality.

It can feel extremely powerful to be associated with *something*. Throughout our lives we regularly hear, "I work for . . . ,"

"I play with . . . ," "I'm a member of . . . ," "I attend . . . ," "I have a deal with . . . ," "We're funded by . . . ," "I'm from . . . ," and so forth.

In short, being associated with a company, team, club, religion, community, band, university, or city provides recognition and a sense of belonging. It's like the permission slip parents have to sign that allows their kid to go on the school field trip. It ensures our right to be part of the pack.

But what happens when this association goes away? What happens when we're laid off or fired? Or, what about when we graduate or when the band breaks up? Or when the season ends? What happens when we branch off on our own and make new choices? This is how we bet on ourselves.

Inherently, there's always something uneasy about beginning a new chapter or carving a new path alone. We've been led to believe that without association or the support of others, we're no longer important. This solitude can make us feel exposed.

We begin to ask questions like "Am I still valuable on my own? Am I still *somebody*?" The short answer is yes, with a big caveat. The same way we endorse political candidates or sports teams, we must be willing to do the same for ourselves.

You must be willing to endorse yourself.

Endorsing yourself means being associated, lovingly, with the person you see in the mirror every day. This sounds simple, but that doesn't mean it's easy. Endorsing ourselves means stepping from the shadows into the light. It means putting ourselves out there in ways that challenge us or make us uncomfortable.

We ask, what will people think if I self-publish a book, start a side hustle, move to a new town, change professions, press Record on my webcam, join a church, travel the world solo, or perform at an open mic? What if I choose the road less traveled and go it on my own? Does this mean I failed?

The real question isn't what people will think if you do it. It's what you'll think of yourself if you don't. This is where a golden opportunity presents itself: the opportunity to be comfortable pursuing our dreams without the endorsements of others and without fear that we'll be judged for our flaws and imperfections.

Your flaws and imperfections are what give you the power to stand alone and endorse yourself.

Most people spend their lives straddling lanes. Half in this lane, half in the other, stuck in the purgatory of in-between. When you endorse yourself, it means that, come hell or high water, you're willing to choose a lane. You make a choice, even if it doesn't end up going as planned.

Even though it might feel like you're walking on a tightrope without a safety net, I'm here to tell you that the safety net has been there all along. I know it feels like you need to find "stability" before you can act, but here's the truth: your mindset, actions, and efforts offer all the stability you'll ever need.

Everything you need to shift your actions from "one day" to "now" is already in your possession. The person who you most need to invest in you, believe in you, support you along the way—is you. The simple fact is that if we don't endorse ourselves, bet on ourselves, no one else will.

You don't have to be exceptional; you just have to be you. That alone is exceptional.

LEAN INTO THE PAIN

Theodore Roosevelt once said, "We must all either wear out or rust out, every one of us. My choice is to wear out."

Though I don't expect you to live your life the same way the twenty-sixth president of the United States did, we still can find inspiration in his life philosophy. There's a major difference between wearing out and rusting out.

Rusting out happens when we do nothing. Wearing out happens when we take action, even if it's painful at times. Everyday life provides us with an opportunity to lean into the pain or lean away from it.

Leaning into the pain means having the tough conversations. It means getting up when you'd rather stay in bed or doing something instead of complaining. It means making the right choice, not the easy choice, and trusting that all will eventually be okay—even when your fear tells you the exact opposite.

Leaning away from the pain means standing on the sidelines of life. It means taking the easy way out. It means treating life like a dress rehearsal as opposed to a real show in front of a live audience.

It's time to change from your practice jersey to your game jersey. Game day is here. It's been game day all along. At some point, we have to put away the personal development books (after you finish this one), hit "pause" on that online course we're taking, and say no to attending another conference. You've been practicing for a long time. It's time to do this thing for real.

How do you become the kind of person who fearlessly leans into the pain? By fully committing and doing the hard work that's required when no one is watching, being prepared, and then, simply surrendering. Trust in yourself. Trust in your decisions. Trust in your path. What's required on your journey of life is ongoing, relentless trust.

BE YOUR OWN BENEFACTOR

I know what you're thinking: Sure, it's easy to say, "Depend on yourself." But I'm not one of those people with deep pockets or a trust fund to lean on. I hear you. I wasn't one of those people either. So, I want to share with you how you can be your own benefactor.

For centuries, artists as varied as Mozart, Pablo Picasso, and Harper Lee have been able to create art because of benefactors. These are people who provide artists with financial support, resources, or whatever else they need so that they can create. These men, women, and foundations come in all shapes and sizes.

These days, creators like bloggers, podcasters, writers, or musicians have different kinds of benefactors to support their work. These include fundraising websites, artist retreats and workshops, or scholarships and grants established by foundations. But to make the most of these, you have to go after them with commitment and vision.

Over the years, I've been lucky enough to have my own benefactors. You may be thinking, *Must be nice, Antonio! I'd love to be in your shoes.* Well, today is your lucky day. Because you see, my benefactors are your benefactors, too. They're called full-time and part-time jobs.

When I first went out on my own as a speaker and coach, the truth is that for quite some time, my income from this work wasn't always enough to provide for my family. So, at times along the journey of building my dream job, I essentially worked a full-time gig on top of all my speaking and coaching engagements.

For a few years, I headed up the higher education division of the personal branding platform *about.me*. For a while, this meant a weekly commute to San Francisco from my home in Los Angeles, on top of my travel for speaking. After that, I led the narrative strategy team at Anatta.io, the top e-commerce agency for health and wellness brands.

I'm grateful for those jobs because they were my benefactors while I got my own business off the ground. It was a bonus that I enjoyed the work and the people at both of those companies. My only regret was that I hadn't publicly shared this truth about my life earlier. The Internet can make everything look glamourous, when the truth behind the scenes is a fourteen-hour shift of hard work.

So many people, people I know, are in the position of building their dream job while working a full-time job, driving for a ride-share company or delivering groceries in the evenings to provide for their family. There should be no shame or stigma in this. Of course, I was once embarrassed to disclose this side of my life—but not anymore. Building a life you love takes courage and hard work.

As Mitch Matthews, the success coach and founder of Big Dream Gathering, once told me:

A dream job is a job that you love or a job that allows you to do what you love.

In other words, you already have what it takes to be your own benefactor. Chances are you're already doing the work. You just have to reframe it.

Being your own benefactor means believing in yourself, investing in yourself, and treating your day job, your employer, and the income that you earn from it as an opportunity to do what you love. It means taking a leap, putting yourself out there, and not being afraid to fund your dreams with your own commitment.

Crowdfunding platforms like GoFundMe, Indiegogo, and Kickstarter help people and organizations raise money for important causes, businesses, and other projects. They could be a good resource for you, too. Unfortunately, some people have allowed platforms like these to paralyze them into believing that they can't start a company, write a book, shoot a short film, or embark on a new journey without the financial support of others.

As individuals, we can learn a powerful lesson from these platforms: we can kick-start ourselves. What did people do before these platforms existed? They invested in themselves—not financially, per se, but with hard work, dedication, and a willingness to stick through the tough times. It all starts with seeing yourself as your own benefactor.

Starting today, kick-start your discipline, your accountability, and the people you surround yourself with. Kick-start your commitment to what you say is most important. And on those days when you're hating your job, your boss, or your commute, always remember it's for a greater cause. You.

EARN YOUR SLEEP

When we become our own benefactor, things start to change for the better. These changes are tangible, and we can feel them in more ways than one.

One metric is how we physically feel at the end of the day. That fatigue you feel, mental and physical: does it feel earned, or does it feel like you're just throwing in the towel after another day? The truth is, far too many of us are going to sleep every night exhausted and feeling like we have nothing to show for it.

*We talk a lot about the importance of a
good night's sleep, but we don't talk enough about
what makes us feel like we've earned that sleep.*

Maybe almost every night you toss and turn in bed. Or, you take a supplement or pills to fall asleep. I used to drink alcohol or NyQuil to fall asleep, only to wake up a few hours later feeling like crap. On the flip side, maybe you're one of those people who go to bed and sleep through the night. But here's the question: when you awake, are you well rested or do you feel like you haven't slept at all?

The reason why so many people struggle to sleep and truly rest is that deep inside they know that they're giving their all to something they don't truly believe in. This gnaws at them to their core, as much as they try to ignore it. Yet each day they wake up and go through the motions again, feeling that metaphorical tap on their shoulder that's trying to show them another way.

Earning your sleep isn't just about closing your eyes at night and keeping them closed until the morning. It's about knowing that every day, even if only in small ways, we are keeping that fire in our belly alive and pursuing our dreams as opposed to simply lulling ourselves into complacency. As a society, we spend way too much time talking about our potential. Potential is useless if you're not taking action.

*Instead of talking about your potential,
start measuring your progress.*

Over the years I've known what it's like to ignore my dreams, my calling if you will. During challenging periods, I struggled to sleep because deep inside, I knew that over the course of my day, and even though I worked full-time jobs, I wasn't putting attention and effort into what I truly wanted to go after. I would give my all to my nine-to-five, but would rarely put energy into what mattered most to me in the mornings before work, in the evenings after work, and during the weekends. I would give my all to everything except me.

The days of putting yourself last are over.

It's time to direct your energy to the things you love, the things that allow you to thrive, and the things that make you human and allow you to feel what it means to live a life on purpose.

These days, when I find myself at a standstill or not making progress on something that matters to me, I think of my days as a track and field athlete. One thing my coaches over the years would always yell is "Run through the finish line!" In other words, don't let up until you finish.

Remember: when you think you're tired or ready to throw in the towel, you can always go a little bit further. You can always do a little bit more. You define the finish line by the effort you give. Life doesn't always have clear "finish lines." Only you can decide where the finish line is.

When you hit that pillow tonight, I want you to know damn well that you earned the comfort of that cozy comforter and those soft sheets because you committed to what's most important. Demand more of yourself. Run through the finish line. You might just surprise yourself.

NEXT STEPS

1. Describe the times in your life when people you
    didn't know very well surprised you by supporting
    you in meaningful ways. Why do you think they
    did this?

2. List five ways that you can regularly endorse
    yourself and become your own benefactor.

3. In what areas of life have you avoided leaning
    into the pain? What would leaning into the pain a
    little bit more each day look like for you?

4. Identify the key things that you can do each day
    to feel like you've *earned your sleep*.

12

THE ROAD MAP AHEAD

*"Don't you think it's time you started doing
what we always wanted."*

—LYRICS FOR "HIGH" BY LIGHTHOUSE FAMILY

SO FAR IN this book, we've explored the mindset, intentions, questions, and steps we must embrace to help us reimagine the rest of our lives. Now, on the following pages, I'm going to provide you with the most practical tips I've given yet. Think of it as a road map that offers direct strategies and specific actions you can regularly take to endorse yourself and make real, meaningful progress in your life.

I intentionally share all of this with you here, toward the end of the book, as we near the end of our journey. That's because what Internet and social media motivational posts fail to tell you is that their strategies and hacks won't work unless you have the necessary foundation to support them. With the guidance in the previous chapters, you've begun to establish this strong foundation. Now these suggestions will help you start to build the life you want in the long term.

The approach I'm about to share works. I've witnessed the results firsthand with my own personal journey, as well as with my coaching clients. Why does it work? The beauty is in the pure simplicity of it. Charting a new path and sparking change doesn't have to be complicated—although we humans are great at making things needlessly challenging.

You may intuitively know much of what you're about to read. However, knowing something and acting on it are two different things. Remember: taking action and being bold begin with a whole lot of work that happens during the unseen hours while no one is watching.

Part of this work is learning to refuel ourselves. In other words, instead of focusing on problems and challenges, we can put our energy toward embracing opportunities for growth, development, and maintenance, if you will. When we do this, we'll find that we can move forward inspired and empowered to kick butt. This mindset is critical. It's what'll keep you going when things get tough—and they will get tough.

THE TOP 5 CHECKLIST

There were difficult periods in my life when my feelings would swing to extremes. One day, I'd feel great and fired up. The next, I'd be in a horrible mood, with little to no energy. It didn't matter the season or time of day. And who was on the receiving end of these bad moods? It was usually family, friends, or colleagues I cared about.

For the longest time, I thought these mood swings were random. But one day, I finally realized that what I'm doing, or rather not doing in my life, plays a profound role in how I show up for myself and others. These days, when I'm not at my best, I start by acknowledging it. Then, I get curious. Next, I do my best not to beat myself up. And finally, I refer to a short checklist to help myself get back on track.

The checklist boils down to five key things that I've learned have a profound positive impact on my life. If I don't do these five things pretty much every day, I can feel the negative effects on my attitude, energy level, focus, and physical and mental health. This isn't just some random checklist—this is *my checklist,* and my clients and I have all come to rely on a personalized version of it. It works for me and I've seen it work for countless others. Does it make every day the best day ever? Nope. But when I am committed to it, I rarely experience the absolute worst day ever.

So, without further ado, here are the "Top 5" things you can do in some shape or form on a daily basis to keep yourself charged and making progress (trust me, you'll thank yourself for it):

- *Learn: The human brain is not designed to stagnate. To that end, finding some outlet for ongoing learning and education isn't just a suggestion—it's a necessity for all of us if we want to keep growing. You can accomplish this on a daily basis by listening to a podcast or an audiobook during your commute; on a monthly basis by completing an online course or by reading a book on a subject you're curious about; and on a yearly basis by seeking out continuing education programs, as well as annual conferences and workshops. Opportunities to educate yourself are not only endless and easy to access, but also essential. (More on this in just a moment.)*

- *Sweat: When is the last time you broke a sweat? Just as our brains aren't designed to stay stagnant, neither are our bodies. Unfortunately, most of us spend most of our days seated at a desk at the office or on the couch at home. Our bodies are craving to move, stretch, and be pushed. It's time to get off your butt, even if only for fifteen minutes, to sweat and release some endorphins. Run, walk, do strength training, take a class at your local gym, kickbox, play tennis, do yoga, chase your kids in the yard . . . just do something.*

When I'm on the road and away from home, sometimes I even open up a fitness app on my smartphone or tablet and get in a twenty-minute workout. Sure, it may be tough to get started. But think of it this way—it's an opportunity to do something that will only make you better. And once you're done, you won't regret having worked up a sweat. You might even learn to love it.

- **Eat.** Most of us think we eat a healthy diet. However, all it takes is tracking our food intake in a journal or on an app for a week to realize we don't eat nearly as well as we think we do. Just as a car needs gasoline (or electricity), you need fuel to be at your best as well. It's critical that the fuel you put in your body in the form of food is an asset as opposed to a liability. If you don't know how to begin eating healthy again, start by reading a book like *Food: What the Heck Should I Eat?* by Dr. Mark Hyman or by following his exceptional and accessible work on social media. Look, I'm not saying that the food you eat has to be organic or gluten-free or dairy-free. But it's critical to consume healthy, nutritious food that gives you energy to perform at your best. Don't rely on those late-night fast-food drive-throughs; they only deplete you.

- **Meditate:** For the longest time, I resisted having a meditation practice. Why? Because I didn't find it easy to sit in silence and be with my thoughts. French philosopher Blaise Pascal's statement that "All of humanity's problems stem from man's inability to sit quietly in a room alone," makes complete sense to me. There's a lot of compelling science that a daily meditation practice can decrease anxiety, increase focus, and improve sleep, even if you only do it for five minutes a day. Plus, there are plenty of meditation apps available to support you. Meditation has morphed from something I *dreaded into a bright spot of my day. As my friend the author and meditation teacher Light Watkins likes to say, "Every day you skip mediation is a win for stress."*

- **Connect:** *Rarely have I ever regretted connecting and having a conversation, short or long, with someone I care about. Though making that phone call or driving in traffic to meet them may seem like an inconvenience, once I hear their voice or see their face, I'm happy I made the commitment to connect. As mentioned earlier in the book, no one who has accomplished anything of significance did it alone. Neither should you. It's critical that on a daily basis, in some shape or form, you truly connect with people who make you happy, challenge you to be better, and hold you accountable. These can be your allies, friends, colleagues, family members, and beyond. My suggestion is that you accomplish this through real-life methods. This means connecting in person, or at least on a phone or video call. It can be as short as five minutes. The important thing is that it's human and intentional.*

- **Bonus tip . . . Journal:** *Beginning or ending your day with a journal entry can be a powerful practice. Your goal can be to write for five minutes uninterrupted, or until you fill up a page with words. You can share what's going on in your brain (the good, the bad, and the ugly); you can capture your wins for the day (what went well and where there's room for improvement); or, you can write down all of the things that you're grateful for (either that day, or more broadly in your life). This "brain dump" is like a detox for the mind.*

This Top 5 checklist is backed up by plenty of research. They might seem like big-time investments at first, but trust me—these activities represent time well spent that makes your life better. Every day, I invite you to actually write these five things down in your daily planner and check them off once they're accomplished. That's how to turn them into a routine. Once you commit to the Top 5, it becomes much easier to take the next key steps that help you ensure your best days are ahead.

START LEARNING AGAIN

Okay, you've got your Top 5 checklist and you're feeling good. Now let's dig deeper into the importance of learning again.

Back in 2013, I regularly hosted online courses with CreativeLive, which offers online courses from the world's top experts, including best-selling authors and experts in topics like business, photography, art, entrepreneurship, and more. One thing I found compelling about CreativeLive is that the students came from all walks of life. These weren't just men and women looking to start new careers or hobbies—these were folks who were committed to lifelong learning, improving themselves, and discovering something new. CreativeLive's free courses provided them with this outlet.

Ongoing education is a critical component of our lives moving forward. After all, the foundation of our lives was built on learning. From grade school to college to maybe even graduate school, we regularly found ourselves in learning environments. During this time, we were exposed to new ideas. We were intellectually challenged. We were regularly tested on what we learned. And then, like clockwork, each semester or school year, we'd be challenged to learn something new again before moving on to the next level.

The challenge in your life now as an adult is that there is no next level. After we complete our formal education, we're thrown into the wild and our education often comes to an abrupt stop. We transition from educating ourselves to showing up for a job and collecting a salary. Sure, some jobs provide a "level" you can attain through promotions, but for many of us, this feels more extrinsically rather than intrinsically rewarding.

The opportunity you have is to become a student again and get yourself back in the classroom—on your own terms. Consider taking a continuing education class at a local college or university. There are tons of free online courses from platforms like CreativeLive and in-person education programs that will teach you pretty much anything you want to know. You can attend one-day trainings or workshops on everything from entrepreneurship to woodworking to computer programming. Want to start smaller? Heck, smartphone apps can help teach you a new language. Always have your eyes open and regularly identify new opportunities for personal growth and development.

FINISH SOMETHING—ANYTHING

In my experience, people are great at starting projects but not so great at finishing them. It's something I've struggled with, too. So, when was the last time you finished something that was important to you? (Binge-watching an Amazon Prime Video series or making your bed this morning doesn't count.)

In 2019, I found myself bored. Even though my hands were full with my family and career, at some point I realized that I hadn't finished anything recently that was just for me. One thing I missed in my life since leaving the television industry was having in-depth conversations with fascinating people. So, I decided to remedy that by starting a podcast, *The Best Thing,* where I talked to people about the best thing to ever happen to them that would never appear on a résumé or come up in conversation. My goal wasn't to get a million downloads or sponsors. Nope. My goal was to interview awesome people and hit Publish each week. Doing this has been a game changer for my happiness and joy. A by-product of this is a devoted community of listeners that love the show.

So, what could you finish? Maybe it's that major home-improvement project. Or one of those books you've been look-ing at on your nightstand for the past year. Maybe it's that 5K race. Or, that large, challenging puzzle that you've wanted to complete for far too long.

Research in positive psychology finds that regular achieve-ment is a critical component of happiness, or to be more spe-cific, thriving in life. It also increases your confidence and your ability to finish stuff again and again. Look over the last few months of your life and identify what you achieved. Now look at the next month of your life and identify one thing that you'd like to achieve or finish. Then, take action.

HAVE SOMETHING ON THE CALENDAR

Like most couples, my wife and I are very different. I've found this to be a good thing. My wife is a planner and loves to have things on the calendar to look forward. This could be weekend dates, vacations, home projects, or holiday plans. Early on, I found all of this scheduling inconvenient and I'd try to avoid making commitments. Today, I find it extremely empowering—so much so that we have a large calendar on our kitchen wall with all of our key family events on it.

When we have something to look forward to on our calen-dar, it motivates us to work toward what's ahead of us. It can even help us get through challenging periods, knowing that good times are ahead. Though some people will say they prefer going with the flow, this approach can often work against you.

Planning ahead and having an agenda allows us to live life pro-actively (as opposed to reactively). When we have something on the calendar, or somewhere to be, it means we're intentional about how we spend our time. In my experience, people who have nowhere to be can end up absolutely anywhere (or nowhere).

Take a look at your personal calendar. Outside of work and the standard weekly obligations, see what you have scheduled. Is there anything on the calendar that really makes you excited? Consider scheduling that next trip or vacation now. Plan ahead to have family or friends over for board game night. Commit to a weekly movie night with your kids. Get those tickets to the traveling Broadway show that's coming to town. Or, plan your next date with your significant other in advance, instead of finding yourself asking, "What do you want to do tonight?" Having something on the calendar doesn't have to be compli-cated. In fact, it can be fun.

CREATE A FUTURE RÉSUMÉ

Speaking of calendars and looking forward, one thing I've never liked about résumés is that they're always looking backward. They share what we've done as opposed to what we can and will do. They highlight our past instead of our aspirations. Don't get me wrong, I get it. Like I mentioned earlier, our past actions can be an indicator of our future successes. But there's an opportu-nity for you to look forward—not just professionally, but also personally—with something we call the "future résumé."

Typically, in a first session with a coaching client, they want to spend energy talking about the past, what's wrong, or what's not working. I kindly remind them that that's not why we're here. In my experience, therapists spend a lot of time focusing on what happened in the past, and that's cool. However, as a coach, my goal and approach is instead to focus on what we'd like to happen moving forward. To do this, I ask questions to get clients thinking ahead and establishing the metrics of what success looks like for them. This approach allows clients to walk away from sessions excited and with a plan, as opposed to dejected from wallowing in the past.

With a future résumé, we can establish what we'd like to be able to say about our lives in areas like our relationships, careers, health, fitness, finances, travel, and beyond. My recommendation is that instead of having your future résumé be one year or five years out, I recommend looking at—you guessed it—the next thirty days.

What would you like to see happen that would make you feel absolutely amazing in the next thirty days? Maybe you'd like to set up two informational meetings to learn about new career trajectories. Or, you could decide to take your kids out on individual "dates" for some one-on-one time this month. It could even just be preparing meals at home to see how much money you save and how much better you eat.

To be clear, we're talking about thirty days so we feel inspired by possibilities, rather than paralyzed by them.

CONDUCT MONTHLY SELF-REVIEWS

As we plot out our future, it's also equally important to press "pause" now and then to regularly review yourself to make sure you're not backsliding or reverting to old, harmful habits. I suggest that you do this monthly.

I've done self-reviews for years. I tend to resist doing them, but I always feel lighter after I finish. Typically, I'll find a place where I won't get distracted, like a coffee shop or park, turn off my phone, and give myself up to an hour to complete it. Here are the five simple questions I ask myself during a self-review (that you can use, too):

1. *What's working in my life?*

2. *What's not working in my life?*

3. *What do I need to stop doing?*

4. *What do I need to start doing?*

5. *What's important about the next thirty days?*

For these questions, I recommend focusing on a key area of your life, like your health, marriage or relationship, career, or finances. To take it a level further, you can share your personal reviews with your spouse, allies, or people you respect that will hold you accountable.

HAVE A PLAN FOR WHEN THINGS AREN'T GOING AS PLANNED

Here's what I know for sure: things aren't always going to go our way and work out as we planned. In our personal and professional lives, things will break, conflicts will arise, and balls will be dropped.

I can still remember some painful and awkward days from my television career. There were times when I'd sit down at home to watch a brand-new episode of a show that I produced for a network, only to realize, seconds in, that I had submitted the wrong version of the episode, one that was not supposed to be broadcast. (Those phone calls with my boss were never fun.) Or, in recent years, I've had a few moments when I'm onstage in front of hundreds of people delivering a speech, and I realize that I submitted the wrong PowerPoint presentation to the conference organizers.

It's in uncomfortable moments like these, when we encounter a specific setback or challenge, that we can ask ourselves four key questions to address mistakes head-on.

1. *What happened?*

2. *Why did it happen?*

3. *What role did I play in it?*

4. *How can I ensure that this never happens again?*

When we honestly answer these questions with ourselves and others with the goal of learning (not blaming), we can get to the root of any problems and make progress. This will help you identify how and where you made errors so you can ensure that you don't make them again. It'll also help you identify gaps in communication, assumptions, and misaligned expectations. You'll learn where you fell short and need to take accountability so you can avoid future challenges—and above all, take ownership of the situation.

MEASURE AND KEEP TRACK

To ensure that you're moving forward and not just standing still, it's critical to regularly measure the progress that you're making in your life. One way to do this is by taking a lesson from chapter 2 on the last thirty days.

At the beginning of each month, I invite you to identify your top priorities. These are the things where there's no gray area, things that can be clearly checked off once they've been accomplished. For example, you can check off if you completed your Top 5 list for 80 percent of the month. You can check off if you had two date nights with your spouse last month. You can check off if you completed your monthly self-review. You can check off the number of times you worked out and built up a sweat. You can check off making time to connect with friends. Identify what's most important and then track and measure it.

REMEMBER WHY YOU'RE DOING IT

Some people just wake up. Others wake up with a purpose. I invite you to be part of the latter group. When we're clear why we're doing something, even on the most challenging of days, we will recommit to what's important.

Some do it for their faith. Many people do it to leave a legacy. Others do it for a social cause. Identify your why and remind yourself of it on a daily basis. Write it on a sticky note and post it to your computer so you see it every day and be thankful that you live in a society where you get to pursue your why.

My why is my family. In those moments of doubt, frustration, or simple laziness, all I have to do is think of my wife and kids to get myself back on track. This energizes me and allows me to push ahead, go above and beyond, and not give up. Every day with the actions I take, I have the opportunity to lead by example and set my family up for success and I do my best to not take this for granted.

13

YOU WERE BORN TO LIVE

*"Think of yourself as dead. You have lived your life.
Now, take what's left and live it properly."*

—MARCUS AURELIUS, *MEDITATIONS*

NOW THAT YOU have your road map and it's almost time for me to leave you, I want this chapter to serve as a reminder that no one can care more about your life than you do. The job of endorsing your dreams and becoming your own benefactor falls on you.

Think about that moment when you're in a room and all the lights unexpectedly go out. For a moment, it's pitch-dark. You can't even see your hands in front of your face. You bump into walls, stub your toes, and walk with your arms extended like a zombie as you attempt to figure out where you are in the space.

Slowly but surely, your eyes adjust to the darkness. It's still dark, but you can see enough to make out shapes, objects, walls, and more.

This accurately describes how many of us have wandered through our lives. It's dark, but we can still see. Maybe we can't see everything, but it's enough to get by.

Then, when the generator kicks in or the power comes back on, the flash of light is a jolt to our system. We can now see *everything* that the darkness had masked.

This book is meant to be the switch that turns the lights back on and allows you to see your life more clearly. We're here to see everything, even if that makes us uncomfortable.

My goal in writing this book is to help you see what's been right in front of you and available to you all along. Once you see your life in this light, you can start to take accountability and responsibility for it.

Of course, even when we see our lives with the lights on and a new awareness of the options before us, one thing is still certain:

Everything's not going to go your way.

You can bet everything on that.

When we accept this truth about life, it can make our roadblocks, setbacks, breakups, and scars that much more bearable.

The challenge is that at times, it may seem like life is going against you more than it's going for you. We've all heard the cliché saying, "It's not happening to you, it's happening *for* you." This is a nice idea, but I'm sure folks facing bankruptcy, divorce, or a serious illness would tend to disagree and say, "Uh, no. This is happening *to* me."

The next inevitable question we ask when we face hardship is "Why me?" But I'm going to challenge you to ask a better question—a question that accountable and committed people ask themselves: "Why not me?"

Like it or not, sometimes things happen to us or fall on our shoulders. Please know that you're built not just to handle this, but also to get through it and beyond.

Maybe your journey would break others. Maybe a family member, spouse, or friend wouldn't make it if they were in your shoes. And that's why they're *your* shoes. Because you *can* make it. Hate it or love it, but you, my friend, are built for this. Deep inside, you are stronger and more equipped than you even know.

The truth is, how we choose to respond to our challenges and adversities determines what our future will have in store for us—even if they don't feel like choices at the time. I know this feeling all too well.

A few years back when my father was diagnosed with dementia, I was experiencing some of the challenges in my personal and professional life that I shared earlier in this book. At a time when I could've used the insight, support, and guidance from my father, I could no longer have a coherent conversation with him. He had lost the ability to talk and we had to move him to a nursing home, where he was bedridden. Seeing the proudest man I know experience this broke my heart. It still does.

As much as I tried to ask myself what I could learn from my father's absence during this tough period in my life, I didn't find any easy answers. Still, I had no choice but to move forward into the light. I had my own young family, and they needed me. Maybe that's what being an adult is: accepting that there are some things you can't change and that you still must live your life in the inevitable face of adversity.

When people say, "It's all about perspective," what they're really saying is:

Find a way to see the light when you're surrounded in darkness. It's always there if you look closely. Just know that when you find the light, it doesn't necessarily make things easier. It just guides your path forward.

IT'S JUST WATER

Of course, sometimes all you need is a healthy dose of perspective, because not all challenges in life are created equal.

During my days as a business journalist, I once found myself walking the streets of Juneau, Alaska. I was in town reporting a story and wanted to get a better feel for the town, community, and culture.

One thing I learned quickly was that, due to the geography of Juneau, it rains a lot there—we're talking more than 230 days a year with some kind of precipitation. The day that I was exploring the town was no different. It was raining and from the looks of the sky, it wasn't going to stop any time soon. So, I borrowed a massive umbrella from my hotel and did my best to stay dry as I walked up and down the streets.

During my walk, I immediately felt like something was off. As I people-watched the locals walking down the street, I realized that no one, except for me, was using an umbrella.

This didn't make any sense to me. I started to feel like I was in an episode of *Black Mirror*. Why wasn't anyone else using an umbrella? What did they know that I didn't?

Being a curious journalist, I walked up to a local to solve this mystery. The guy I approached wore an old work jacket and eyeglasses. His glasses were covered with small beads of water from the rain, though it didn't seem to bother him one bit.

"Excuse me, sir," I said, grabbing his attention. "I'm not from here."

He looked at me and said, "I can tell."

"I noticed that no one here is using an umbrella," I continued. "Why is that?"

Bemused, he looked at me and my large umbrella. Then, he

took a step closer to me and said, "You know man, *it's just water.*"

Before I could respond, he walked away.

It's just water.

Holy moly. Those three words hit me in such a powerful way. On a literal level, on a philosophical level, and on an existential level. For that moment, with those simple three words—*it's just water*—everything in my life made complete sense.

Indeed, many of the challenging times that we experience are just water. Rain is temporary. Eventually, the water will dry. But in the meantime, we must really feel the rain and let ourselves get wet. Then, and only then, can we experience the sunshine—if we remember to seek it out.

The sunshine won't always find you. Sometimes, you have to step outside and find it.

Life is often about how we frame the situations we encounter. To be sure, we're all going to experience trying times: a health diagnosis of a loved one that turns our world upside down, or a job that comes to an unexpected end. There will be wildfires, floods, global pandemics, and so much more that's out of our control. But we get to determine if our path forward will be one of grace and ease, or one of resistance and pain.

In our lives, there are moments when someone or something is offering us sunshine—or at least shelter from the rain. Are you open to seizing these moments? Are you open to finding the sunshine? Are you ready to come in out of the rain, dry off, and start fresh?

THE PLACE WHERE YOU GO TO GIVE UP

Of course, at some point when we find ourselves getting soaked, we'll be tempted to give up on something. It could be a career, relationship, business, project, or something else that's important to us.

When we find ourselves in this state of mind, typically what we do is go to a place that makes it easier for us to give up. We'll go to a bar and throw back a few drinks. We'll spend time with thieves of ambition who support our misery. We'll lock ourselves in our homes, far away from people who care about us. We'll help Amazon's stock price stay high by purchasing stuff we don't need to distract us. We'll scroll through social media on our phones until our thumbs are numb. Or, maybe we'll stuff our faces with "comfort foods" that do the exact opposite of comforting us.

Throughout my life, during times when I've wanted to give up, I've closed myself in closets and reached for alcohol, marijuana, TV shows, quesadillas and tortilla chips, seclusion, and people who always distracted me. Before you go to that place where it's easy to give up on what matters, I encourage you to reconsider. There's another way.

Years ago, one morning I was walking around the Nicaraguan surf town of San Juan Del Sur, where I hosted the Ignition Lab retreat. I stumbled into a café seeking some solitude and Wi-Fi. But right away, I knew something didn't feel right.

The interior of the bar contrasted with the beautiful pastel colors of the town and the crisp ocean air. Outside it was sunny, fresh, and clear. Inside it was dark, dank, and smoky.

Though it wasn't yet 10:00 a.m., the bar was full of expats nursing alcoholic drinks and chain-smoking cigarettes. All of the people at the bar looked tired, worn out, and depressed. *People didn't come here to seek free Wi-Fi*, I thought. *They came here to give up.* Sure, maybe I was passing judgment. But when you see the place where people go to give up, you can feel it in your gut.

Somehow, I knew that the longer I stayed in this small version of my hell on earth, the worse I'd feel. I mean, I even found myself ready to grab a drink and bum a cigarette from someone to join the "give up club." But instead, I hightailed it out of there.

Immediately after stepping outside into the sun, it felt like a heavy weight had been lifted off my shoulders. In an attempt to boost my spirits, I sought out another café, and I found one just a few doors down.

This café was the exact opposite of the first one. It was bright and airy. The walls and the music were colorful. The patrons wore smiles on their faces. Instead of just booze, they served fresh-squeezed juice, coffee, and herbal tea. Instead of cigarette smoke choking the air, the scent of nag champa incense drifted in.

My energy level immediately spiked. I exhaled in relief. Who knew that what I needed was just a few doors down?

Sometimes during rough patches, when it's easy to give up,

we must be careful where and how we spend our time and energy. It's easy to find the dark places where we're surrounded by our vices—like the closet I once smoked weed and drank beer in. We're drawn to them like powerful magnets, whether they're substances, people, or environments that take energy away from us.

But if we're patient and willing to walk a few doors down, we can find the perfect place that energizes us, where people support us, and where we feel empowered. This is the place where we're catapulted to be the best version of ourselves.

> *Right now, in this very moment, you can make a decision that could ruin your life. Also, in this very moment, you can make a decision that could improve your life.*

It's always your choice.

BORN TO LIVE

For me, nothing changed my definition of *home* more than becoming a father—that is, becoming the person who was creating a home for someone else. I quickly learned how profound this is.

When my wife and I had our twins, they were born premature at thirty-two weeks. Our son and daughter each weighed fewer than four pounds and they had to spend weeks in the neonatal intensive care unit at our local hospital.

Watching our children struggle early on was one of the hardest things I've ever had to experience. As they fought to build their strength over the course of weeks, even with setbacks, each day they got stronger. They had a fight in them that reminded me of what makes us human. It became obvious to me that our twins, and we—all of us—are born to *live*. Today, our twins are healthy, thriving, and succeeding at wearing me out.

The past few years have had their share of highs, lows, and everything in between. However, I'm proud to report that I no longer hide in alleys, smoking Camel Crush Menthol cigarettes while wearing a bright green gardening glove. I don't have it all figured out, but I've come so far from where I was in my life, marriage, and career, and I continue to make positive strides. Each day I'm committed to making it better than yesterday.

I still face challenges. I'm tested on a daily basis, and some days I want to throw in the towel and quit. But I don't. I always remind myself not to make a permanent decision over a temporary circumstance.

It doesn't matter if other people think you have it all figured out. What matters is what *you* think about how you choose to live your life. This means choosing to recommit to your standards as opposed to the ebb and flow of your emotions.

As we come to the end of this book, I invite you to take stock of all that you *do* have. All that you have experienced—both the good and the bad. And all that you can and will experience and do in the future.

Realize that you have the power, everything inside of you, to make necessary changes to fill your life with purpose and reignite that fire inside you.

In the midst of your journey, always remember that there's nothing to feel guilty about. If no one else has ever told you this, allow me to be the first:

Your happiness hurts no one.

Please allow that to sink in with all of your being.

Of course, it won't be all happiness all the time. It won't all be perfect. But every day, you have the opportunity to learn from the bumpy roads you encounter. You have it within you to brush yourself off from falls and bounce back.

Be warned that you'll regularly encounter people who are fighting their way through life. The choice you get to make is living life open, always ready with a hug, versus living it with a clenched fist, always ready to fight.

Don't fight your way through life, celebrate it.

Celebrate every day when "not much" happens. The average Tuesday. Making your kids' breakfast in the morning. Going grocery shopping. Going for a walk with friends or family. Taking out the garbage. These are things that people describe as "not much." What I've come to realize is that "not much" is actually EVERYTHING. Those "not much" moments are THE moments.

Don't wait for a special occasion to celebrate. Make today a special occasion. Open up that great bottle of wine on the shelf. Wear that new dress or suit that makes you look and feel fabulous. Don't wait until someone's birthday to celebrate them.

As we move forward, when you talk about the "good old days" my hope is that you're talking about today. The good old days are now, waiting to be lived. You create them with your choices, attitude, and actions. After all, the best thing to happen to you is still ahead of you.

END HERE ◀

IF NO ONE else has said it to you lately, allow me to say, I'm proud of you.

When you first opened this book, odds are you were at a crossroads in your life. You had a decision to make. A choice to keep living as you were with all of the old stories, or to chart a new direction.

You decided to bet on yourself and leave the old stories behind. I applaud your courage.

Far too many people give up right as their blessing is about to take place. On the days when you're ready to give up, instead I ask you to trust.

Life is about the choices you do and don't make. Never forget that not making a choice is still, in fact, a choice.

Life is about either taking responsibility and accountability for our actions, or making excuses.

Life is about commitment. Every day we have to recommit to what's most important, even when things aren't going our way.

Life is about being present and in the moment—not being

stuck in the past or far ahead in the future, but instead taking in all the beauty that is with us now.

Life is about being proactive, not reactive. "Winging it" is easy when you're well prepared.

Life is about belief. Believing in ourselves the way others believe in us and having faith.

More than anything, life is about love. The more love we give, the more successful we will be in all facets of our life.

Always remember, we must also be willing to receive love. To do this, we must do what many never will: love ourselves.

Never forget that your happiness hurts no one. Don't dim your light for anyone, especially yourself. It's okay to be happy.

It's more than okay to shine. In fact, happiness looks good on you.

Live life on purpose. When in doubt, just go back to what you most want. This will always keep you on track.

Oh, and don't forget to smile. None of this counts unless you're having fun.

So, go ahead. Live your life. We need you.

Antonio Neves
Los Angeles

ACKNOWLEDGMENTS

No one who has accomplished anything of significance did it alone. That's truly the case with this book. The words you read wouldn't have been possible without the help, support, guidance, and love of so many amazing people and places. It would be impossible to thank everyone. So if you've been on this journey with me, I thank you from the bottom of my heart.

To my agent, Cynthia Zigmund, what an amazing journey we've been on. Thank you for believing in me and this project through all of the iterations. I'm so glad Debra Englander introduced us.

To my editor Michele Eniclerico and the team at Harmony/Rodale, thank you for the "red ink" and for helping to make this book the best it could be. It's an honor to be publishing this book with you.

To my friend, personal editor, and fellow twin parent Shiwani Srivastava. I couldn't imagine doing a project without you. Thank you for the care, attention to detail, and joy you bring to each project.

To my friends who have supported me on this book journey, I don't know where I would be without all of you. Jon Gordon, thank you for taking the time on that flight in 2015 to help me outline the first ideas for this book. Mitch Matthews, thank you for being an amazing coach, mentor, and friend (and of course, the officiant at my wedding).

Much love to the Man Morning crew of Cal Amir, Chris Girbés, Mohit Jain, Mark Leibowitz, Dhru Purohit, Nirav Sheth, Dileepan Siva, and Corey Sousa. Our time together each week has been nothing short of life-changing. Dhru, you have consistently gone above and beyond with your time and knowledge—I appreciate your generosity.

Jess Ekstrom, thank you for all of the encouragement, expertise, and motivation. Sam Davidson, thank you for the metaphor support and your sense of humor. Dan Charnas, thank you for reminding me to stand up for myself and for always appreciating when it's 2:00 pm. Laila Al-Arian, thanks for being an amazing friend since day one of J-School. Our next coffee is on me. To Vanessa and Lydia, thank you for being family to me. I miss you two. DFetts and McNeil—since our New York City days, you two have always had my back and I appreciate that. Our group text messages make me laugh way too hard. Lincoln Stephens, thank you for always sharing the perfect encouraging word or message when I need it most. Bassam Tarazi, man, I could write a whole chapter based on our conversations. But for now, I'll just say you're a gem, bro, and you make me better. Aaron Oaks, thanks for being the epitome of a best friend and for always having your boy's back. (Would you be mad if I forgot to thank you?)

To my family, thank you for always rooting for me. Tony and Paty Kouba, thank you for your generosity. Bobby Thompkins and Beverly Neves, thank you both for being far more than stepparents to me. Narvell Neves, thank you for the idea of becoming your own benefactor and for being such an amazing cousin. Shawn Wiley, thank you for always being in my corner.

I aspire to match the level of kindness and care you show to others. Nick Neves, I'm glad you're my big brother. Let's go fishing! Kenyetta Lewis, your little brudder loves you. Thanks for your support with the twins. Dad, thanks for the powerful life lessons you've taught me. I miss you. Mom, I could write a whole book just for you—but for now, thanks for loving and always encouraging your "Mr. Midget" and liking all of my posts (and for helping to watch the kiddos).

To my son, August and daughter, Harper, I'm so glad I'm your Dad. You make me proud. You two truly are my "best thing." To my wife, Brigitte, thank you for all you do for our family. This book wouldn't have been possible without your support, encouragement, and countless rereads of the book to help make it better. Words can't express my appreciation for all you do. I love our family.

ENDNOTES

START HERE

1. "State of American Well-Being: 2017 Community Well-Being Rankings," Gallup-Sharecare, March 2018, https://wellbeingindex .sharecare.com/wp-content/uploads/2018/03/Gallup-Sharecare -State-of-American-Well-Being_2017-Community-Rankings _vFINAL.pdf.

CHAPTER 3

1. "Facts and Statistics," Anxiety and Depression Association of American, 2018, https://adaa.org/about-adaa/press-room/facts-statistics.

CHAPTER 4

1. "Time-Sensitive Clues about Cardiovascular Risk," Harvard Health Publishing, Harvard Medical School, March 2019, https:// www.health.harvard.edu/heart-health/time-sensitive-clues-about -cardiovascular-risk.

CHAPTER 5

1. Guy Trebay, "The New York Cool of Dao-Yi Chow and Maxwell Osborne," *New York Times,* September 9, 2016, https://www.ny times.com/2016/09/09/fashion/mens-style/new-york-cool-dkny -public-school-dao-yi-chao-maxwell-osborne.html.

2. Joseph Luciani, "Why 80% of New Year's Resolutions Fail," *U.S. News and World Report,* December 29, 2015, https://health.usnews .com/health-news/blogs/eat-run/articles/2015-12-29/why-80-per cent-of-new-years-resolutions-fail.

3. Kate Zernike and Jeff Zeleny, "As a Minor Senator, Obama Showed Star Power," *New York Times,* March 9, 2008, https://www.ny times.com/2008/03/09/world/americas/09iht-obama.4.10847495 .html.

CHAPTER 8

1. Scott Hankins, Mark Hoekstra, and Paige Marta Skiba, "The Ticket to Easy Street? The Financial Consequences of Winning the Lottery," *Review of Economics and Statistics* 93, no. 3 (August 2011), https://www.mitpressjournals.org/doi/abs/10.1162/REST_a_00 114#.VpLMM1J327Q.

2. "Surfers only Spend 8 Percent of the Time Riding Waves," SurferToday, n.d., https://www.surfertoday.com/surfing/surfers-only -spend-8-of-the-time-riding-waves.

CHAPTER 10

1. News release, "New Cigna Study Reveals Loneliness at Epidemic Levels in America," Cigna, May 1, 2018, https://www.cigna.com /newsroom/news-releases/2018/new-cigna-study-reveals-loneliness -at-epidemic-levels-in-america.

2. Vivek Murthy, "Work and the Loneliness Epidemic: Reducing Isolation at Work Is Good for Business," *Harvard Business Review,* September 2017, https://hbr.org/cover-story/2017/09/work-and-the -loneliness-epidemic.

3. Francie Hart Broghammer, "Death by Loneliness," Real Clear Policy's America Project, Pepperdine School of Public Policy, May 2019, https://www.realclearpolicy.com/articles/2019/05/06/death _by_loneliness_111185.html.

4. "Relationships and Good Health the Key to Happiness, Not Income," London School of Economics and Political Science, December 13, 2016, http://www.lse.ac.uk/website-archive/newsAnd Media/newsArchives/2016/12/Relationships-and-happiness.aspx.

INDEX

ABOUT THE AUTHOR

Antonio Neves is an internationally recognized speaker, success coach, and award-winning journalist. He regularly delivers keynotes and trainings at top organizations worldwide. Antonio hosts the international chart-topping podcast, *The Best Thing*. For over ten years, Antonio worked as a business correspondent, host, and producer with top television networks. As a journalist, he has spent hundreds of hours interviewing and profiling prominent CEOs, startup founders, politicians, entertainers, athletes, and beyond. A first-generation college graduate, Antonio is a graduate of Western Michigan University and earned his master's degree from Columbia University.

Unlock Reader Exclusives
Stoplivingonautopilot.com
Enter the code: BEST

Connect with Antonio on Social
Instagram: @TheAntonioNeves
Twitter: @TheAntonioNeves
Facebook: @TheAntonioNeves

Speaking
For speaking inquires and to sign up for my email list, please visit:
www.theantonioneves.com